D0929979

TWAYNE'S WORLD AUTHORS SERIES

A Survey of the World's Literature

Sylvia E. Bowman, Indiana University

GENERAL EDITOR

ARGENTINA

John P. Dyson, Indiana University

EDITOR

Jorge Luis Borges

(*TWAS 108*)

TWAYNE'S WORLD AUTHORS SERIES (TWAS)

*The purpose of TWAS is to survey the major writers
—novelists, dramatists, historians, poets, philosophers,
and critics—of the nations of the world. Among the
national literatures covered are those of Australia,
Canada, China, Eastern Europe, France, Germany,
Greece, India, Italy, Japan, Latin America, New Zea-
land, Poland, Russia, Scandinavia, Spain, and the
African nations, as well as Hebrew, Yiddish, and
Latin Classical literatures. This survey is comple-
mented by Twayne's United States Authors Series
and English Authors Series.*

*The intent of each volume in these series is to present
a critical-analytical study of the works of the writer;
to include biographical and historical material that
may be necessary for understanding, appreciation,
and critical appraisal of the writer; and to present all
material in clear, concise English—but not to vitiate
the scholarly content of the work by doing so.*

Jorge Luis Borges

By MARTIN S. STABB

University of Missouri

TWAYNE PUBLISHERS

A DIVISION OF G. K. HALL & CO., BOSTON

Library of Congress Catalog Card Number: 77–110704

ISBN   0–8057–2168–1

MANUFACTURED IN THE UNITED STATES OF AMERICA

Contents

Preface

Few if any writers of the contemporary Spanish-speaking world have gained the acclaim now enjoyed by Argentina's Jorge Luis Borges. The simple fact that international criticism has taken note of a modern author whose language is Castilian is in itself unusual. This interest, moreover, has not been merely perfunctory. During the past two decades translations of Borges' work have attracted steadily increasing critical attention in France, the United States, and elsewhere.

The recognition Borges now enjoys was gained by writing only relatively short poems, short essays, and short narratives. If one were to apply a purely quantitative standard, it might be said that Borges has written no "major" works. What has attracted the most attention to him, especially on the part of foreigners, are his almost unclassifiable *ficciones:* precisely structured narratives, frequently based on a philosophical idea, in some respects akin to the traditional short story, and in others, to the essay. A few volumes of these *ficciones,* together with several substantial collections of essays and poems constitute Borges' primary literary production. In addition, he has written a large number of secondary pieces: book reviews, minor articles, prefaces, introductions to literary texts, and so on. He has also collaborated on occasion; the most significant of these joint enterprises is his work with his friend Adolfo Bioy Casares—a writer of detective and fantasy fiction. Finally, Borges' role as a literary catalyst must be noted. As an editor of important literary reviews, as a model for younger writers, or even as a literary value against which less-established writers might react, Borges has come to exert a very strong influence upon Argentine—and Spanish American—letters of this century.

The present study is an attempt to introduce the work of this fascinating and complex writer to North American readers. While several books about Borges have appeared in Spanish, only two, one of which is based on a Spanish original, have been published in English. In both studies the authors have emphasized Borges' prose fiction rather than his over-all literary production. The present work, by contrast, endeavors to point out Borges' main themes as they become manifest in his poetry, his essays, and his prose fiction. This organizational scheme thus provides the opportunity to analyze some of the formal aspects of Borges' literary art, as well as philosophical and esthetic concerns.

All of Borges' major writings—his collected poems, his essays, and his stories—were carefully examined preparatory to the writing of this book. In addition, the author read a good many of the minor writings noted above. However, it must be made clear that no attempt has been made to incorporate all of these minor works into the present study.

In order to make this volume more helpful to nonspecialists and especially to North American readers, an introductory chapter on Borges' life and times has been included. The final chapter, on Borges and the critics, will perhaps raise as many questions as it answers, for Borges is not an easy writer to assess. His position as the leading Argentine—if not leading Spanish American—writer of the midcentury has not gone unchallenged. A number of his compatriots, particularly the younger writers, have characterized his work as gratuitous, "de-humanized," as clever, but content-less. There are, perhaps, some grounds for these charges. And, as we shall see in the closing pages of this study, a full airing of the case for and against Borges leads directly to the most basic kind of question regarding the nature of literary art and the role of the writer in today's world.

A substantial amount of Borges' prose, and some of his poetry, has been translated into English. Where published translations have been quoted in the text, their source is indicated: all other translations are my own.

MARTIN S. STABB

Columbia, Missouri

Chronology

1899   Born, August 24, Buenos Aires. Son of Jorge Borges and Leonor Acevedo de Borges.

1914   Travels with his family to Europe. At outbreak of World War I, is forced to remain in Geneva, Switzerland, where he attends secondary school.

1919   Travels in Spain. Publishes several poems under influence of Spanish *Ultraísta* movement.

1921   Returns to Buenos Aires. Collaborates on "billboard review" *Prisma*. Edits the manifesto "Ultraísmo" published in magazine *Nosotros*.

1922   With several others, founds the review *Proa*.

1923   Second trip to Europe. Publishes first collection of verse, *Fervor de Buenos Aires*.

1924   Founds, with others, the second *Proa*.

1925   Publishes *Luna de enfrente* (verse) and *Inquisiciones* (essays).

1926   Publishes *El tamaño de mi esperanza* (essays).

1928   Publishes *El idioma de los argentinos* (essays).

1929   Publishes *Cuaderno San Martín* (verse) and receives Second Prize in Municipal Literary Contest.

1930   Publishes *Evaristo Carriego* (essays).

1932   Publishes *Discusión* (essays).

1935   Publishes first collection of narrative prose, *Historia universal de la infamia*.

1936   Publishes *Historia de la eternidad* (essay).

1937   With Pedro Henríquez Ureña publishes *Antología clásica de la literatura argentina*.

1938   Death of Jorge Borges, his father. Takes post as assistant librarian in small municipal library. Late in year, suffers accident and is hospitalized for several weeks.

1940   With Silvina Ocampo and A. Bioy Casares publishes *Antología de la literatura fantástica*.

1941   Publishes first major collection of stories, *El jardín de senderos que se bifurcan.* With Silvina Ocampo and A. Bioy Casares publishes the *Antología poética argentina.*

1942   The magazine *Sur* dedicates special issue to Borges on the occasion of his not being awarded the National Prize for Literature. With A. Bioy Casares publishes humorous detective stories, *Seis problemas para don Isidro Parodi* (under joint pseudonym, H. Bustos Domecq).

1944   Publishes *Ficciones* (stories). Receives "Prize of Honor" from the S.A.D.E. (Sociedad Argentina de Escritores).

1946   With Bioy Casares publishes *Dos fantasías memorables* and *Un modelo para la muerte* (stories) under pseudonym, H. Bustos Domecq. Under pseudonym B. Suárez Lynch publishes anthology, *Los mejores cuentos policiales.* Renounces post of inspector of poultry and rabbits given him by Perón government as reprisal for his criticism of regime.

1947   Publishes *Nueva refutación del tiempo* (essay).

1949   Publishes *El Aleph* (stories).

1950   Publishes *Aspectos de la literatura gauchesca* (essay).

1951   Publishes *La muerte y la brújula* (stories); with Delia Ingenieros, *Antiguas literaturas germánicas;* and with Bioy Casares the second series of *Los mejores cuentos policiales.*

1952   Publishes *Otras inquisiciones* (essays).

1953   Publishes with Margarita Guerrero, *El Martín Fierro* (essay).

1955   After fall of Perón is named Director of the National Library. Publishes in collaboration with Bioy Casares, *Los orilleros* and *El paraíso de los creyentes* (unproduced screenplays) as well as several minor collaborations. Named member of the Argentine Academy of Letters.

1956   Appointed Professor of English Literature at University of Buenos Aires. Receives honorary doctorate from University of Cuyo. Awarded National Prize for Literature.

1957   With Margarita Guerrero publishes *Manual de zoología fantástica.*

1960   Publishes *El Hacedor* (verse and short prose). With Bioy Casares publishes anthology, *Libro del cielo y del infierno.*

1961   Shares International Publisher's Prize (Prix Formentor) with Samuel Beckett. Publishes *Antología personal* (prose and poetry). Invited to teach in United States at University of Texas. Travels and lectures in United States.

1963   Travels and lectures in England, France, Spain, and Switzerland.

1967   In September marries the former Elsa Astete Millán (widow of Ricardo Albarracín Sarmiento). Invited to teach at Harvard University as Charles Eliot Norton Lecturer. Travels and lectures in the United States.

1968   Returns to Buenos Aires.

CHAPTER 1

Borges: The Man and His Times

BORGES once observed that there were two kinds of writer: those whose literary career was a mere episode in an otherwise worldly and active life and those whose writing was in fact the entire expression of their existence. Borges himself clearly belongs in the second category. Except for some teaching and for his directorship of the Argentine National Library, he has devoted himself completely to writing. Moreover, his biography has little significance or interest except as it marks the trajectory of his remarkable literary career.

I   Early Life and Travels

Jorge Luis Borges was born on August 24, 1899, in Buenos Aires. The Borgeses were a well established, financially comfortable *criollo* family whose antecedents could be traced back to the wars of independence. One branch of the family—that represented by his paternal grandmother, Fanny Haslam—was English. Borges' father, a writer, jurist, and a student of modern languages, apparently knew English well as did young "Georgie"—as Jorge Luis came to be called. Borges did not attend school until he was nine; his education was entrusted to an English tutor, a Miss Dink. His father, too, played an important part in shaping his son's nascent literary interests. Borges' earliest memories go back to the family home in the Palermo district of Buenos Aires and more specifically to "a garden . . . and a library of limitless English books." It was here that Borges first whetted his literary appetite on narrations of adventure in distant lands—Robert Louis Stevenson and Kipling were among his earliest favorites. Friends of the family recall the young Borges' odd fascination with exotic beasts, especially the Indian tiger—an animal whose image and metaphor was to haunt many a page of the mature writer. A recent Argentine book on his work even reproduces a sketch of a tiger which "Georgie" drew (in a book of English nursery rhymes) at the age of four.[1] Borges' acquaintance with Hispanic literature came after his early exposure to English letters. This fact is not surprising in view of his family's cultivation of things English and considering the relative paucity of juvenile literature in Spanish. The first Argentine works which he read as a boy were Eduardo Gutiérrez' gauchesque adventure novels—a literary genre rather like the North American "dime Westerns" of yesteryear. As a child he also tasted the more customary fare of the Hispanic tradition: classic works such as the *Quijote* and the epic of the *Cid*.

His childhood seems to have been relatively placid and pleasant. The warmth of Borges' boyhood recollections is obvious to any reader of his work, particularly to those who know his poetry. Family life—in typical Latin fashion—was close-knit and protective. His sister Norah was a constant companion; his relationship with his grandparents, especially with his English grandmother, was warm. Visitors came to the Borges household frequently, and many were men of considerable literary stature. Some of these family friends became personal and literary deities in the eyes of the young Borges; one such friend, the poet Evaristo Carriego, exercised a lifelong influence on him, an influence rather disproportionate to Carriego's intrinsic literary worth.

Shortly before the start of World War I the Borgeses visited Europe. The war broke out while the family was in Geneva, where they remained until 1918. Borges has recalled his stay in Switzerland with fondness; his friend and biographer, Alicia Jurado, describes him enjoying his first taste of French language and letters, studying German at the local school, and spending long afternoons rowing on Lake Geneva with Norah. During this period Borges' literary appetite appears to have been voracious: he read Hugo and Baudelaire in French, Heine and the works of the nascent Expressionists in German. While in Switzerland Borges also discovered two authors who came to occupy central positions in his thought: Schopenhauer and Chesterton.

With the end of the war, the Borges family continued their European travels. In 1919 they visited Barcelona and then Majorca. For some three years following the family traveled on the Spanish mainland, residing in Seville and Madrid.

Borges' first real literary efforts are a number of poems, composed during his Spanish travels. However, he considers the work of this period (1919–21) to be inferior, and has permitted only a very few of these pieces to be reprinted in collections of his poetry. The Spanish writers whom Borges met and with whom he collaborated were a colorful group of young experimental poets, the so-called *Ultraístas*, Guillermo de Torre, Rafael Cansinos Assens, and their followers. Viewed as a European literary movement, *Ultraísmo* shared much of the spirit of its contemporaries: Dada, the Surrealists, and perhaps the Expressionists. From the strictly Hispanic viewpoint it was a prolongation of the reaction against nineteenth-century poetic values—especially Spanish Romanticism—which an earlier group, the poets of '98, had initiated. But like all young Turks the Spanish *Ultraístas* seemed especially bent on proving the literary worthlessness of the generation which immediately preceded them. The exact nature of this movement and of its impact on Borges' work will be discussed later: of greater interest at this point is the picture of the young Argentine which his Spanish friends supply. Cansinos Assens describes the twenty-year-old Borges as "smiling, full of discreet serenity, urbane, even-tempered, with a poet's ardor held in check by a fortunate intellectual coldness; having a classical culture of Greek philosophy and Oriental troubadors making him fond of the past . . . of Latin dictionaries and folio manuscripts, but without making him deprecate modern wonders. . . ." [2]

II *The Poet and His City*

The family returned to Buenos Aires in 1921, an event which unquestionably moved Borges deeply. Despite his fondness for Europe and for the culture of the Old World, Borges' feelings toward his country and especially toward his native city have always been characterized by a profound and almost filial love. The frequently cited lines of his poem, "Arrabal" ("Neighborhood"), written the year of his return, gives some indication of these sentiments: "The years that I have spent in Europe are illusory, I have always been (and shall always be) in Buenos Aires" ("los años que he vivido en Europa son ilusorios, yo he estado siempre [y estaré] en Buenos Aires.") [3]

The Argentina which the Borges family found upon their return differed from the country they had left. By 1914 Buenos Aires had passed the 1,500,000 mark: though the war temporarily halted the

steady stream of immigration which had been flowing toward the
Río de la Plata, with the end of the conflict the city resumed its
phenomenal growth. The economy, despite the brief postwar
slump, was changing and expanding. New industries—mining and
petroleum exploitation—were developed during the period of
wartime isolation and provided the basis for an accelerated program of modernization. The famous Buenos Aires subway, still in
the early stages of construction when Jorge Borges departed for
Europe with his family, was now complete and in operation.
Buenos Aires' characteristic low, sprawling skyline was being
modified. The traditional one- or two-story residence—complete
with patio and landscaping—persisted, although six- and seven-
story buildings were becoming increasingly common.

The craze for modernity and cosmopolitanism was everywhere
in evidence. Yet curiously, a number of picturesque, typically Argentine institutions flourished in the burgeoning metropolis.
Among these, the cult of the tango seems especially strong. The
1920's saw this sensual though sentimental dance emerge from the
slums and brothels to the most elegant cabarets of the downtown
district. Gardel, the composer and singer, an almost mythic figure
in the world of tango, presided over the cult. Despite the subway,
the glare of electric lights, and the gleaming new construction, the
individuality of many of the old neighborhoods (the *barrios*) was,
at least for a time, preserved. Like a small town within the metropolis, Palermo, Belgrano, or Avellaneda had their own tree-
lined streets, quiet patios, bars, dancehalls, intimate cliques, and
local gossip. In a sense, *barrio* life was a prolongation of nineteenth-century Argentina into the more dynamic, higher-pressured
world of the twentieth. As such it exercised a great charm on
the young Borges, who after an absence of seven years no doubt
felt out of step with a Buenos Aires that no longer conformed
to the pattern of his childhood memories. The lovely poems
of his first collection—centered as they are on the patio, the
older sections of the city, the quiet retreat of parks and cemeteries
—are clearly products of his desire to capture the essence of a
world that was fast disappearing.

The new spirit of the postwar era was especially manifest in
politics. In 1916, Hipólito Irigoyen, the shining hope of the Radical party, was elected to the presidency. A growing middle-class,
election reform and the extension of suffrage had paved the way

for the defeat of the conservative oligarchy that had virtually controlled the country for some twenty-five years. But the Radicals, purporting to represent the middle and lower-middle classes, had only an ill-defined program and a candidate who eventually proved less than competent. Fortunately for the new administration, the economy was healthy during most of the decade which followed the close of World War I. As a result, the Radicals succeeded in holding the presidency throughout the 1920's, despite a number of problems—student agitation, the 1919–20 slump, and occasional labor troubles. Marcelo T. Alvear, a lackluster chief executive whose policies resembled the "business-as-usual" approach of his North American contemporary, Calvin Coolidge, sat in the Casa Rosada for the six-year term beginning in 1922. Irigoyen became president again in 1928. At age seventy-five, his incompetency had become even more obvious than it had been during his first administration: in 1930, when the economic bubble burst, he and his party were overthrown and Argentina fell into the hands of a military-Conservative coalition which controlled her destiny until the rise of Perón in the mid-1940's.

One wonders if Borges' rather apolitical attitudes would have been different had his youth not been spent abroad and had his formative years been spent in an atmosphere of greater political responsibility. Many Argentinians, including the intellectuals of Borges' circle, viewed the ineptness of the Radical party with mild amusement, cynicism, or with plain indifference. As an example of a middle-class progressive movement it was a frustrating failure, yet neither Irigoyen nor Alvear had the infamous proportions of a Rosas or Perón. However, it would be misleading to attribute Borges' apolitical position merely to external circumstance. Even in his earliest writings he makes clear that he is not—to use a present-day writer's phrase—a "true believer." Borges has neither the pretensions of those who claim to know ultimate truth, nor the faith of those who will hold to a religious or political credo, even though proof is wanting. A note of ineffectiveness haunts his work in that he seems unconvinced that either he as an individual, or that man in general, can understand what is objectively real. It follows that we can do very little about altering the external world. Significantly, his early poetry is shot through with adjectives such as "vain," "futile," and "undermined." For Borges, the writer's essential role is one of observation, of analysis, and especially of deciphering the symbols that give us a hint of the obscure, conjectural forces that shape reality but which lie just beyond our ken. Moreover, Borges seldom speaks of originality or creativity. He believes that writers, and perhaps men in general, merely rearrange that which is given and immutable. These notions are hardly those of the political activist. If they support any political position, it is a mild conservatism or, as it was called in the nineteenth century, liberalism. Consistent with these attitudes, he has written approvingly of Herbert Spencer and of the need in Argentina for a political party promising "the strictest minimum of government." [4] Yet as a private citizen Borges has definite political opinions: he has consistently opposed totalitarian regimes, though this opposition does not usually appear in his work. While his supporters consider this omission to be in keeping with his temperament and with his philosophy of literary art, some of his critics consider it unforgivable.

By the early 1920's Borges' career commenced in earnest. Together with a group of young writers rather like his Spanish circle, he undertook the publication of a literary review, the writing of poetic manifestos and most important, the polishing of a distinctive poetic style. His first venture, the review *Prisma,* is indicative of his group's mood and orientation. A "magazine" of art and poetry, *Prisma* was not circulated in the usual manner; instead it was prepared on large sign paper and then plastered on walls and fences. It was a gift to the people of Buenos Aires. As one of Borges' collaborators proclaimed "We have bedecked the streets with poetry, we have illumined your path with verbal lamps, we have girded your walls with vines of verse!" [5] There is a certain joie-de-vivre in this gesture; a certain youthful playfulness which Borges has retained over the years. For the Argentine *Ultraístas* of the early 1920's, literature was a game, a pleasant and rather aristocratic sport for bright young sophisticates. The formal tenets of the movement (emphasis on metaphor, free rather than rhymed verse, and the elimination of superfluous poetic adornments) are made clear in the "Ultraist Manifesto," edited by Borges and published in the magazine *Nosotros,* a bastion of the literary establishment.[6] Yet as a well-defined movement *Ultraísmo* was short-lived, though its spirit lingered on. Argentine writers who held to a position of social commitment in literature were, and continue to be, cool toward the group; for unlike some of the European movements of the vanguard, the *Ultraístas* were —as writers—politically aloof, ambivalent in their assessment of human progress, and decidedly not Marxist. Though he may have shared some of these general attitudes, Borges repudiated the formal tenets of *Ultraísmo* almost as soon as he began publishing his poetry.

The mid-1920's was an active period for Borges. Three major collections of poetry were published in 1923, 1925, and 1929, respectively, while his first collection of essays, *Inquisiciones* (*Inquiries*) appeared in 1925, followed by *Tamaño de mi esperanza* (*Dimension of My Hope*) in 1926. Following the ephemeral "mural-review" *Prisma*, Borges joined forces with a somewhat different group in order to publish another literary magazine, *Proa*. More significant than the journal itself was Borges' association with several new writers, the most influential of whom was the eccentric humorist-philosopher Macedonio Fernández. To appreciate this relationship fully it is necessary to read the edition of Fernández' work which Borges lovingly prepared years later (1961). Significantly, one of the things he singles out in discussing his friend's work was the fact that "those who are called intellectuals today are not really so, since they make of their intelligence a job, or an instrument for action." ("Quienes hoy se llaman intelectuales no lo son en verdad, ya que hacen de la inteligencia un oficio o un instrumento para la acción.")[7] But Borges notes, "Macedonio was a pure thinker. . . . He possessed to a high degree the arts of inaction and solitude." ("Macedonio era un puro contemplativo . . . poseía en grado eminente las artes de la inacción y de la soledad.")[8] Borges accepted other aspects of Macedonio Fernández' curious view of the world and of intellectuals, as we shall note later.

Late in 1923 Borges again traveled to Europe, visiting England, France, and Spain. His trip to Madrid was marked by the appearance of a highly laudatory article on his poetry in Ortega's renowned journal, the *Revista de Occidente*. The author of the article, Ramón Gómez de la Serna, was one of several important Spanish writers who were just becoming acquainted with Borges and his work. Another was the young critic Guillermo de Torre, the husband-to-be of Norah, Borges' beloved sister and close companion since childhood.

One of the most interesting periods in Borges' literary life began in 1924 when, on his return from Europe, he began writing for the satirical avant-garde review *Martín Fierro*. His association with the *Martinfierrista* group is significant. This group held to views of art for art's sake, of literature as "diversion" rather than as an instrument for social criticism and amelioration. Another clique of writers, chiefly those who gathered about certain leftist journals, formed the opposition—espousing what would today be called literature of commitment. Curiously, the two bands, the more effete literary aristocrats of the *Martín Fierro* (known also as the *Florida* group) and the so-called *Boedo* group on the left, knew each other well and were often close friends. Those familiar with the Buenos Aires literary scene of the mid-1920's have even suggested that this "division" of the city's young writers into opposing camps was little more than a deliberate and consequently superficial imitation of European literary factionalism, if not a mere joke. Borges made no direct contribution to the literary polemics between the two groups, yet his compatriots are loathe to forget that he was a *Martinfierrista:* they have always assumed that his writing should reflect the playful, aristocratic, and "disengaged" attitudes of the group. Whether or not this assessment of Borges is valid is a question that may only be answered after his multiform work is examined.

To search for dramatic or significant events in the personal life of Borges is remarkably unrewarding: his entire existence has been so inextricably linked with his writing that a "pure" biography of the man would make dull reading. Borges, moreover, is essentially a shy and reserved person who prefers not to speak of his personal affairs. Interviewers typically report that any questions they ask about his nonliterary activities are either shunted aside or answered in literary terms. Though his writings do reveal something of his private life, the information gleaned in this manner is hardly abundant. One can deduce, for example—on the basis of certain poems in his early collections—that during the 1920's and early 1930's he was seriously interested in several women, one of whom he apparently loved deeply.[9] An indication of Borges' reserve is seen in the fact that he has suppressed a number of the more amorous poems of his first editions in the collections of his poetry published more recently.

III   *The Mature Writer*

Since the mid-1920's the main events in Borges' life with only a few exceptions, have been the writing of books. In 1938, following the death of his father, Borges took a minor post as a municipal librarian. This position helped bring out the bibliophile that seems to have always been latent in his nature and probably helped accelerate his growing blindness. At about this time Borges shifted his literary interest from poetry and the essay to prose fiction. Earlier, in his *Historia universal de la infamia* (*Universal History of Infamy,* 1935), he had taken the first hesitant steps in this direction: but the highly imaginative, typically Borgesian fantasies for which he became world famous, did not begin to appear until 1939.

Alicia Jurado, a student of Borges' work and one of his personal friends, notes that Borges suffered a severe fall during Christmas of 1938. He struck his head in the accident and was subsequently hospitalized for several weeks; she points out that it was only after this traumatic event that he began to write such celebrated fantasies as "Tlön, Uqbar, Orbis Tertius." Although Jurado hesitates to affirm a concrete link between these events, she does consider them important enough to be mentioned.[10] At any rate, during the following decade Borges did produce the bulk of his *ficciones.* Although he continued to write essays and poetry, it was the appearance of such startling collections as *El jardín de senderos que se bifurcan* (*The Garden of the Forking Paths,* 1942), *Ficciones* (1944), and *El Aleph* (1949) which attracted worldwide attention to him. Translations of his work began to appear in the United States, and with the return of a group of French exiles who had been in Buenos Aires during the war, Borges' fame spread across the Atlantic.

At home Borges did not fare so well. His *Jardín de senderos que se bifurcan* was nominated for the National Literary Prize in 1941, but to the chagrin of his supporters, a much inferior writer won the award. Borges' friends reacted sharply: the influential literary magazine *Sur* devoted almost an entire issue to a "Vindication of Borges" while the following year Argentina's leading literary club, the S.A.D.E. (Sociedad Argentina de Escritores) established its own literary prize which was awarded to Borges in 1944.

This very prolific period in Borges' life coincides with a steady deterioration in Argentine morale. The economic depression of the early 1930's, followed by the specious boom of the 1940's, an ambivalent attitude toward World War II, and a steady drift away from political democracy mark the decade and a half which culminated in the dictatorship of Juan Perón. The typically rigid and reactionary Conservative Party ruled the nation from 1930 until the military takeover of 1943. During the following two years Perón, from his vantage point as head of the Argentine Department of Labor, built a solid base of popular support among the lower and lower middle classes. Capitalizing upon this group's distrust of the traditional military oligarchy, their economic frustrations, and their cynical attitudes toward the machinery of democracy, Perón became the most powerful force in the nation. Nonetheless, most observers of Argentine politics agree that his election to the presidency in 1946 was legitimate. Ironically, one of Argentina's most honest elections paved the way for one of her most repressive dictatorships. The details of Perón's consolidation of power are well known: the new Constitution of 1949 gave him an unprecedented free hand in the nation's affairs as well as the right to succeed himself; the early 1950's saw him intervene in university affairs and seize control of the nation's newspapers; finally, in the waning years of his regime, he struck out against the church, one of the few remaining obstacles lying in his path to complete domination of the country.

The position of the intellectuals, especially of the writers during this period of the erosion of Argentine democracy, has not been fully studied. It is true that some of the leading literary men spoke out against the drift toward totalitarianism, others participated in a kind of mute protest, while a few were outright supporters of Perón and his program. It is difficult to say how effective the intellectuals might have been had they adopted a more active role and formed a solid bloc of opposition to Perón or to his predecessors.

Though essentially an apolitical person, Borges did take an unequivocal stand against the dictatorship. Early in 1946—just before the election of Perón—he signed a petition criticizing the military regime then in power. As a result, Perón relieved him of his post of municipal librarian and offered him a job as "Poultry Inspector for Fairs and Exhibitions." His refusal of this insulting offer was celebrated at a dinner held in his honor and at which he publicly delivered a stinging attack on the cruelties and stupidities of dictatorship. A number of other facts underscore the genuineness of his political convictions. During the high point of Perón's regime he accepted the presidency of the markedly anti-Peronist S.A.D.E., and throughout this period he earned his living by teaching and lecturing at private rather than government-supported institutions. There is no doubt, then, that Borges opposed the tyranny; yet he remained in the country and continued to write. Perhaps the highly imaginative fantasies of these years were produced in response to the unpleasant realities of the times. Yet Borges seldom, if ever, injects overt political criticism into his work. Those who feel that writers are obliged to take an unequivocal stand on specific political, social, or economic issues, and that they are then obliged to propagandize these views are usually very disappointed with Borges. They do not realize that for Borges the times in which we live, troubled as they may be, are not unique, and that the writer who cries out most loudly against injustice, evil, and cruelty may indeed be only feeding his shaky ego. A similar problem is posed by Borges' attitude toward Argentina—her destiny, her essence, her uniqueness. The bulk of contemporary Argentine writers, as well as Latin Americans in general, have addressed themselves directly to this search for "essence," be it *Mexicanidad, Peruanidad,* or *Argentinidad.* Borges, by contrast, has not participated very actively in this quest. There are good reasons for this apparent aloofness, just as there are valid reasons—at least in terms of Borges' own philosophy and temperament—for his apolitical stance. These matters lead directly to the core of the critical problems surrounding Borges; as such they will be taken up later in this survey of his work.

With the fall of Perón in 1955, Borges' fortunes rose. Official recognition of his merit came in the form of his being named director of the National Library and, in the following year, of his appointment as professor of English literature at the University of Buenos Aires. The literary production of the preceding five years, highlighted by the publication in 1952 of the essay collection *Otras inquisiciones (Other Inquiries),* was crowned by his being awarded the National Prize for Literature for the year 1956. Borges has maintained a brisk tempo of literary and scholarly activity throughout the post-Perón decade. Despite his increasing blindness he published several books in collaboration with his friend, Adolfo Bioy Casares, and with others. His interest in Germanic literature, especially the older Scandinavian and Anglo-Saxon literatures, continues unabated. Moreover, during the past ten years his poetry—often overlooked by all except Borges scholars—has appeared regularly. The past decade has seen Borges become an international figure: he won the Paris International Editors Prize in 1961;[11] he taught as visiting professor at the University of Texas; he traveled extensively in Europe and North America; and he appeared in an increasing number of French, English, and German translations. At this writing (winter, 1968) he is lecturing at Harvard University.

Until 1967 Borges lived quietly in Buenos Aires with his aged but remarkably alert mother, who served as his secretary, reader, and constant companion. The bond between the two was undoubtedly strengthened by Borges' blindness and by his innate shyness. Those who knew the Borges family well were always impressed by the relationship between mother and son: Mrs. Borges' frequent references to "Georgie," her meticulous catering to Borges' every need, and her management of his public appearances all created a picture of maternal concern that struck some observers as charming and others as rather amusing.

Several times during his life Borges seemed to have been on the brink of matrimony. On at least one occasion, during late 1964 and 1965, it was rumored that he had in effect married. Though these rumors proved false, Borges—ironically a writer who constantly maintained that there could never be anything new under the sun—did marry in 1967 at the ripe age of sixty-eight. His wife is the former Elsa Astete Millán, an attractive widow some eleven years his junior. Borges' acquaintance with her dates from 1927, when the two met at the home of the critic and literary historian, Pedro Henríquez Ureña. Although the future Señora Borges, then only seventeen years old, was quite taken with the young author, she married another man, Sr. Ricardo Albarracín Sarmiento, shortly thereafter. Widowed in 1964, her old friendship with Borges was renewed: they were finally married on September 21, 1967, "just at the start of the Argentine Spring," as Mrs. Borges fondly recalls.

IV   *The Man Behind the Book*

The temptation to analyze Borges' literary personality in terms of familial relationships is great. There is much of the little boy who has never grown up in his makeup. His toys may be sophisticated ones: bits of an ancient Gnostic cosmology or a book review of a nonexistent volume, but the manner in which he plays with them suggests an essentially juvenile spirit. In a somewhat different way, Borges' poetry shows a similar mood but blended with the nostalgia of age. His verse reveals a yearning for familial protection, for the tranquillity and serenity of the patio, the garden wall, the mellow luster of old mahogany furniture; in short—a desire to remain forever the child, surrounded by things he knows well and by people who accept him for what he is and without reservation.

Given this aspect of Borges' personality, it is not surprising that he shuns public exposure and guards his privacy jealously. He frustrates the efforts of interviewers and even of acquaintances who try to pry too deeply into "the real Borges." On such occasions, he is courteous, witty, playful, but essentially evasive. His characteristic technique to avoid revealing himself is to steer the conversation toward literary matters. Alicia Jurado, a friend who has worked with Borges, dined with Borges, visited museums with Borges, strolled through miles of Buenos Aires with Borges, sadly confesses that "during all these hours over the course of a ten-year friendship, we spoke, interminably, about literature." [12] James Irby, who was fortunate enough to have a long interview with Borges early in 1962, reports that Borges consistently shunted personal questions aside but that when conversation turned to matters of literature, thought, and language he showed an "almost infantile ingenuous enthusiasm." Irby states his over-all impression of Borges in succinct terms: "As no other writer whom I have known, Borges *is* his works." [13] Another interviewer, Pedro Gómez Valderrama, is in basic agreement—talking with Borges is a "confirmation" of what one deduces about the man from his books rather than a revelation of a "different" Borges. When another interviewer, Gloria Alcorta, tried to get Borges to speak about his love life, he replied that he'd always loved women, but that he had deliberately chosen to keep his amorous interests private and hence the theme is infrequent in his works. As Borges slyly put it,

"I have been too preoccupied by love in my private life to speak of it in my books." [14]

It is ironical that some critics, dazzled by Borges' erudition, have considered him an egoist or "a self-proclaimed genius," to use one writer's unkind epithet. A careful study of his works and a careful examination of the evidence presented by people who know him well, indicate that these detractors misread his basic personality. There certainly may be valid grounds for criticizing his work and even for rejecting Borges' underlying notion of literary art, but to attack him for being an egoist is simply a confession of ignorance.

Borges, by contrast, is shy, rather introverted, and quite uncomfortable when speaking about himself. He apparently prefers to be judged by his works—to be discussed as Borges the writer rather than as Borges the man. Since the events of his life are not especially dramatic while the content of his works is, this attitude makes good sense. Yet there is another important aspect of Borges' disinclination to discuss his personal affairs. Borges, as his work reveals, questions the very idea of individual uniqueness. True, he respects great men, and he has his personal gallery of literary heroes, but he rejects hero worship, the cult of the personality, and all forms of egocentrism. For Borges, the world is too infused with chance for us to take pride in our individuality. The traitor, but for a turn of the wheel, could have been the patriot, and vice versa. Moreover, in the astounding repetitions of history one life parallels another (or prefigures another, to use his favorite term) to the extent that the biographies of two men often blend completely. These notions are consistent with his belief that there is nothing new under the sun. This conviction colors much of his thinking about the world, about politics, about human nature, and most of all, about Borges.

CHAPTER 2

Borges the Poet

BORGES became famous as a writer through his prose rather than his poetry. Even today—especially among his foreign readers—he is thought of first as the creator of fictional labyrinths, as the writer of erudite short essays, often on arcane subjects, and only lastly as a poet. Yet he began as a poet and has worked more or less continuously in this genre. Most important, he reveals more of himself in his verse than in any other kind of writing. The capriciousness, the learned frivolity and playfulness of much of his prose are rarely found in his poetry. By contrast we see in it the other Borges—the sincere and ardent youth of the 1920's or the contemplative and nostalgic writer of the 1950's and 1960's. For many this is an unknown Borges; perhaps it is the real Borges.

Borges' career as a poet and writer began when he was in his late teens. His travels in Europe and contact with the Spanish avant-garde has already been noted. It will be recalled that just after the close of World War I he became acquainted with a group of rising Spanish poets: Rafael Cansinos Assens, Gerardo Diego, Guillermo de Torre, and others. These men, the *Ultraístas,* were at the time little more than adolescents. They were approaching manhood in a Spain which seemed untouched by the war, isolated from the rest of Europe, and just beginning to stir from the slumber of centuries. The *Ultraístas* craved innovation and were repelled by the tastes of their fathers. Where the previous generation preferred the rich musicality of rhyme, the younger men would write in blank verse; where the poets of the 1890's sought a mood of sentimental decadence, the new poets would be playful and sportive; and where the older writers roamed a poetic landscape of ancient palaces, swans, and royal gardens, the *Ultraístas* would plunge themselves into the here and now. It was under the stimulus of such ideas that the young Borges began writing poetry. These early efforts are quite varied.

In some pieces he indicates the trajectory he would travel later: others follow alternate routes which lead nowhere in terms of his future development. A few pieces dealing with the horrors of the war and inspired by the German Expressionist poets exemplify the latter, while the poem "Aldea" ("Village"), published first in the Spanish magazine *Ultra*, and one of the few early poems published in the *Fervor de Buenos Aires*, presents a twilight scene, and certain key words typical of his later work. But Borges has never considered the bulk of these early poems, published in ephemeral Spanish literary journals, as worthy of preservation: he has excluded all but a few of them from his later collections and anthologies.

Modernism, the principal target at which both the Spanish and Argentine *Ultraístas* were aiming, is the logical point of departure for any historical consideration of Borges' poetry. The movement, certainly one of the very major trends in Hispanic literature, had dominated Spanish American poetry since the early 1890's. In Argentina its vigor can be ascribed to the poetic genius of two men. The first, Rubén Darío, was a Nicaraguan but had spent some of his most productive years in Buenos Aires: students of Hispanic literature in both Spain and Spanish America consider him to be the father of the movement and one of the very few genuine poetic innovators in the language since the Golden Age. The second, Leopoldo Lugones, was a native Argentinean, who after coming under Darío's spell, soon developed a very personal, richly imagistic poetry of his own. Darío reached the high point of his career at about the turn of the century; Lugones, about a decade later. Darío, a diplomat and journalist, became more important as an international figure, while Lugones became the dominant personality in Argentine Modernism. He outlived Darío by many years and continued to publish substantial poetry through the 1920's and into the 1930's.

It is difficult to generalize about a literary movement as complex as Modernism. In a sense, when Darío and his followers began their literary revolt they were continuing a century-old tradition of Romantic rebellion. Their emphasis on the autonomy of art, their upholding of the poet's right to express himself in terms consistent with his own temperament, their denial of universally valid literary precepts, and their image of themselves as men at odds with their environment, all underscore the essentially Romantic nature of their movement. Yet one of the *Modernistas'* chief goals was to do away with Romanticism—that stereotyped, imitative Romanticism, which at least in the Hispanic world, had persisted as the lifeless remains of a once-vigorous body. They set about to accomplish the task in a variety of ways. Formally, they experimented with long-forgotten meters which antedated the Romantics, and when these were found lacking, new ones were invented. They tried to replace the tired adjectives of the early nineteenth century with new and unusual ones: as Darío proclaimed, "the adjective which does not give life, kills" ("el adjetivo que no da vida, mata"). The *Modernistas* also sought to blend, confuse, and interchange the distinct sensory realms in their poetry. Following the French poets Baudelaire and Rimbaud, they attempted to establish "correspondences" between sound and color. Taking the Parnassians as a point of departure, they tried to create verbal statuary in which the precise tactile and visual terms replaced the Romantics' overt egocentrism and emotive vocabulary. From Verlaine they acquired the notion that words possess an inherent musical quality which might be the very essence of poetry.

The content of Modernist poetry, like its form, differed substantially from the literature that preceded it. The newer poets preferred the artificial, where the Romantics glorified the world of nature. They held to theories of detachment and objectivity, where the Romantics exalted the ego and cultivated literary confessionalism. The poets of the 1890's shunned overt political or social involvement, where many of their predecessors were activists and reformers. The Modernists, like the Romantics, enjoyed decorating their poetry with the trappings of a distant age, but when they sought escape into the past their favorite periods were the Renaissance and the Classical age in contrast to the Romantic love of the medieval. Finally, the typical Modernist tried hard to avoid the Romantic's penchant for the picturesque: hence he did not concern himself with the Indian, the *patria,* or with local color. Instead he wrote of the courts of Versailles or of the sensuous refinement of ancient Greece. Though the Modernists imitated their European mentors to a great extent, their poetry—particularly the best pieces of the leading writers—had much originality. For certain members of the movement, Modernism proved to be a means rather than an end: for these poets, and Lugones could justifiably be included among them, it served to free the writer from the clichés and constraints of midcentury Romanticism and to direct him toward richer and more personal modes of expression.

The exact chronology of Modernism is difficult to establish, but during the first decade of the present century, the innovations of Darío, Lugones, and their followers began to lose some of their appeal among younger Hispanic poets. By the time Borges was in Spain, a full-blossomed reaction against *Rubendarismo* had developed. Since the Modernist tide had engulfed Spain as well as Latin America, it is not surprising that the Spanish *Ultraístas* participated as actively in this reaction as did their counterparts on this side of the Atlantic. Yet it would be inaccurate to claim that Borges' poetry—even of the early *Ultraísta* period—was merely a reaction to Modernism. It is true that he wished to purge his poetry of certain specific Modernist techniques and mannerisms, but like all good poets his objective was to affirm his own poetic values rather than refute those of his predecessors. Borges admits that he never adhered to the position he sketched out in his "Ultraist Manifesto" of 1921. The points he emphasized are nonetheless worth enumerating: the reduction of lyricism to metaphor; the combining of several images in one; and the elimination of adornments, sermonizing, and all forms of poetic filler. A corollary to his view that poetry must be purged of unnecessary embellishments was his conviction that rhyme and meter contributed little to the value of a poem.[1]

Borges was less explicit about the thematic materials which *Ultraísmo* was to employ, but in general he favored contemporary rather than antique poetic furnishings. He even proclaimed that the poets of his generation prefer the beauties of a transatlantic liner or of a modern locomotive to the magnificence of Versailles or the cities of Renaissance Italy. This statement is only half serious: what he meant was that the here and now—the immediate environment—is the logical point of departure for creating genuine lyricism and that the overuse of highly decorative trappings typical of *Modernista* poetry detracted from true lyrical expression and impeded the poetic process.

I   Fervor de Buenos Aires

At first glance the forty-five short pieces of free verse in Borges' first collection seem to be little more than a group of vignettes describing familiar scenes in and around his native city.[2] However, to say that *Fervor de Buenos Aires* is a group of poems describing the city of Buenos Aires, would be equivalent to saying that Keats's "Ode to a Nightingale" is a poem about a bird. As in all good poetry the presence of one kind of thematic material or of another is of secondary importance. What matters is how successfully the poet communicates a particular mood, an affective state, or a fleeting insight—in short, how he transmutes the everyday world into the poetic realm.

It is true that about half of the compositions employ thematic materials drawn from Borges' observation of Buenos Aires' streets, gardens, cemeteries, and buildings. A few pieces, by contrast, present exotic scenes: "Benarés" describes the Indian city of the same name; "Judería" ("Jewry"), the ghetto of an unspecified but obviously European city. One poem, "Rosas," takes as its point of departure the figure of Argentina's tyrannical nineteenth-century dictator. A limited number of poems are purely introspective and as such they do not describe any specific external reality. The poems vary from seven or eight lines to as many as fifty, with fifteen to twenty lines being about the average. In keeping with *Ultraísta* precepts, neither regular meter, rhyme, nor regularized strophes are in evidence. The absence of traditional forms does not mean that these poems have no structure: like other writers of free verse, Borges does incorporate formal devices into his poetry. The effectiveness of these devices will be better appreciated after Borges' poetry is examined in greater detail.

The mood of the *Fervor de Buenos Aires* is established in the opening lines of the first poem, "Las calles": "The streets of Buenos Aires/have become the core of my being./Not the energetic streets/troubled by haste and agitation,/but the gentle neighborhood street/softened by trees and twilight . . ." ("Las calles de Buenos Aires/ya son la entraña de mi alma./No las calles enérgicas/molestadas de prisas y ajetreos,/sino la dulce calle de arrabal/enternecida de árboles y ocaso . . .")[3] Despite the word "Fervor" in the collection's title, the reader soon becomes aware that this is a restrained fervor, a reflective passion directed toward an internalization of all that surrounds the poet. This goal is best achieved by selecting that portion of reality which is most easily assimilated: not the bustling downtown streets, but the passive, tree-shaded streets of the old suburbs. It may be a valid generalization to say that in all his writing, Borges seeks out the passive and manageable facets of reality in order to facilitate the creation of his own internal world. A random sampling of the modifiers used in the *Fervor* bears the point out: Borges writes of "trees which barely mutter (their) being" ("árboles que balbucean apenas el ser");[4] of the "easy tranquility of (the) benches" ("el fácil sosiego de los bancos");[5] of the "fragile new moon" ("la frágil luna nueva");[6] of "withered torches" ("macilentos faroles");[7] "the obscure friendship of a vestibule" ("la amistad oscura de un zaguán");[8] of the ray of light which "subdues senile easy chairs" ("humilla las seniles butacas")[9] in an old parlor; and of "streets which, languidly submissive, accompany my solitude" ("calles que, laciamente sumisas, acompañan mi soledad").[10] Borges' frequent use of the late afternoon as a poetic setting may have a similar function. Aside from the obvious fact that the beauty of sunsets and the coming of night have always appealed to writers, the dulling of reality's edges at this time of day gives the poet a special advantage in his task of shaping the external world.

One cannot help wondering why the young Borges felt a need to infuse reality with these qualities of passivity and submissiveness. Perhaps his innate shyness, coupled with the experience of foreign travel and subsequent return to the half-familiar, half-alien scenes of his childhood led him to view the world with trepidation and insecurity. His vocabulary throughout the *Fervor* is revealing. It clearly indicates that he is seeking tranquillity, familial solidarity, and a kind of serenity which can only be associated with parental protectiveness. Examples are abundant: in "Las calles" he speaks of the neighborhood streets as providing "a promise of happiness/for under their protection so many lives are joined in brotherly love" ("una promesa de ventura/pues a su amparo hermánanse tantas vidas");[11] in "Cercanías" ("Environs") he writes of "neighborhoods built of quietness and tranquillity" ("arrabales hechos de acallamiento y sosiego");[12] and in the beautifully understated final verses of "Un patio" he sums up the peace and serenity of the traditional Latin residence by exclaiming

"How nice to live in the friendly darkness/of a vestibule, a climbing vine, of a cistern" ("Lindo es vivir en la amistad oscura/de un zaguán, de una parra y de un aljibe").[13] The most complete expression of this theme appears in the poem "Llaneza" ("Frankness"). Borges begins the piece by describing his opening a garden gate "with the docility of a page that one turns devoutly and frequently" ("con la docilidad de la página/que una frecuente devoción interroga").[14] Once within, he does not have to notice physical objects, for they are already fixed in his mind's eye. Most important, he feels no need to prove himself, no need to seek special privileges: everyone knows him, his troubles, and his faults. In a word, he is accepted without reservations into the protective warmth of the home. Borges' own words carry his message best: "This is reaching the highest good,/That which, perhaps, we will attain in heaven:/Neither admiration nor acclaim/But simply to be admitted/As part of an undeniable reality,/Like stones or trees" ("Eso es alcanzar lo más alto,/lo que tal vez hemos de conseguir en el cielo:/no admiraciones ni victorias/sino sencillamente ser admitidos/como parte de una Realidad innegable,/como las piedras y los arboles").[15]

Closely related to Borges' poetic transmutation of "hard" reality into a pliable, manageable reality is his recourse to a certain philosophical notion which has come to occupy a central position in all his work. In "Caminata" ("Stroll"), one of the less anthologized poems of *Fervor*, he writes: "I am the only viewer of this street, if I would stop looking at it, it would perish" ("Yo soy el único espectador de esta calle,/si dejara de verla se moriría").[16] In "Benarés," superficially one of the least typical pieces in the collection, Borges describes in considerable detail a place which he has never seen. He admits in the opening lines that the city is "False and dense/like a garden traced on a mirror" (Falsa y tupida/como un jardín calcado en un espejo").[17] Yet at the very end of the poem he seems amazed that the real Benares exists: "And to think/that while I toy with uncertain metaphors,/the city of which I sing persists" ("Y pensar/que mientras juego con inciertas metáforas,/la cuidad que canto persiste").[18] In a better known poem, inspired by the Recoleta cemetery, he observes that when life is extinguished "at the same time, space, time and death are extinguished" ("juntamente se apagan el espacio, el tiempo, la muerte").[19] What Borges is driving at in these poems is made ex-

plicit in another piece, "Amanecer" ("Daybreak"). The poem is
set in the dead of night, just before daylight appears: with "the
threat of dawn" ("la amenaza del alba") the poet exclaims, "I
sensed the dreadful conjecture/of Schopenhauer and
Berkeley/that declares the world/an activity of the mind,/a
(mere) dream of beings,/without basis, purpose or volume"
("Resentí la tremenda conjetura/de Schopenhauer y de Berke-
ley/que declara que el mundo/es una actividad de la mente,/un
sueño de las almas,/sin base ni propósito ni volumen").[20] In the
rest of the poem, Borges follows out the logic of Berkeleyan idealism. There is a brief moment, he writes, when "only a few night-
owls maintain/and only in an ashen, sketched-out form/the vision
of the streets/which later they will, with others, define" ("sólo
algunos trasnochadores conservan/cenicienta y apenas bosque-
jada/la visión de las calles/que definirán después con los otros").[21]
In this moment in which few or no mortals are maintaining the
universe, "it would be easy for God/to destroy completely his
works" ("le sería fácil a Dios/matar del todo su obra!").[22] Berkeley, as a corollary to his idealism, posited God as the maintainer of
the universe—if and when there might be no human beings available to perceive and hence to guarantee its existence. But Borges
injects another thought into the poem, and one which is alien to
Berkeleyan philosophy. He suggests that there is some danger
that God might choose to take advantage of this brief period
when the universe hangs by a thread. The implication here is that
a capricious, vindictive, or negligent God may actually wish to
destroy the world. Rather than in Berkeley, the source for this
notion is to be found in Gnosticism, a philosophical current that
has shaped much of Borges' thought. "Amanecer," at any rate,
ends on an optimistic note: dawn comes, people awake, God has
not chosen to destroy the world, and "annulled night/has remained only in the eyes of the blind" (". . . la noche abolida/se
ha quedado en los ojos de los ciegos").[23]

This poem, as well as the other poems in *Fervor* which deal
with the Berkeleyan refutation of matter, poses a basic problem in
the approach to Borges. One might ask, as some critics have done,
whether Borges really took these ideas very seriously. Does it
make any sense for a person in the twentieth century to be concerned about the world disappearing because no one is awake to
perceive it? Did Borges actually fear that a malicious God was

about to destroy our universe, or perhaps let it perish by default?
This seems unlikely. Rather, he appears to have been toying with
an idea and not expressing the fears of a tortured soul. He has
often indicated that philosophical notions, religious doctrines, and
mathematical concepts hold merely an esthetic appeal for him. It
is in this sense that his manipulation of Berkeley's ideas must be
understood. The infectious logic of the eighteenth-century philosopher caught Borges' fancy and, although he really was not terribly worried about the full implications of Berkeley's thought, he
could not resist the temptation to play with this new toy. Yet we
shall see that Borges' almost childish love for the intellectual game
must not be taken as a sign of insincerity, nor as an indication that
he is incapable of deep feelings.

Two of Borges' best-known essays, written years after the poetry
of the *Fervor*, are intriguingly titled "Historia de la eternidad"
(1936) and "Nueva refutación del tiempo" (1944–47). In both of
these pieces, as well as in many other essays, stories, and poems,
Borges' preoccupation with time is most apparent. With a host of
other writers past and present Borges shares the very human desire to stop time, to restore the past, or to dispel the fears of the
future. In the everyday world, we know that to do these things is
impossible, yet poets have always felt that their peculiar sensitivity to time may, in some way, permit them to accomplish these
miracles. There are, moreover, certain occasions when the desire
to "refute" time is especially strong. Borges found himself in just
such a situation in 1921, when after a seven-years absence, he returned to a Buenos Aires greatly changed by the passage of the
years.

Certain words and phrases which crop up in his poetry of the
early 1920's illustrate Borges' intense desire to check the flow of
time. The verb *remansar* (to dam up, to create a backwater or
eddy) and its related adjective *remansado* are not particularly
common terms in the Spanish poetic lexicon though they appear
several times in the *Fervor* and occasionally in later collections.
Borges writes of an "afternoon which had been damned up into a
plaza" ("la tarde toda se había remansado en la plaza");[24] of a
dark, old-fashioned bedroom where a mirror is "a serene backwater in the shadows" ("una remansada serenidad en la
sombra");[25] of doomlike solitude "dammed-up around the town"
("La soledad . . . se ha remansado alrededor del pueblo").[26] The

significance is obvious: if time is a river, then the poet is seeking the quiet backwaters where time's flow is halted. Though Borges' fascination with time has often been interpreted as an example of a purely intellectual exercise, the very personal sources of this interest should not be overlooked. The traumatic return to Buenos Aires as well as the essential inwardness of his personality clearly help account for the emphasis on this theme in his early work.

In addition to the *remanso* motif, the *Fervor* contains other fine examples of Borges' reaction to the rush of time. He begins the poem "Vanilocuencia" by stating "the city is inside me like a poem/which I have not succeeded in stopping with words/" ("La ciudad está en mí como un poema/que no he logrado detener en palabras").[27] Though words, especially in the form of poetry, seemingly "freeze" or "pin down" the flow of time, Borges is aware of the crushing fact that the objects of the world are "disdainful of verbal symbols" ("desdeñosas de símbolos verbales")[28] and that despite his poetry every morning he will awake to see a new and changed world. The futility of trying to check the flow of time by literary creations, by recalling the past, or by surrounding oneself with old things appears clearly in the *Fervor* and has since become a dominant theme in all of Borges' writing. Yet his attitude is ambivalent and leads to a poetic tension for he knows that time—in the brutally real, everyday sense—flows on, that the world will change, that Borges will grow old, and that the past is forever gone. Yet he is reluctant to give in without a struggle, though he knows his efforts are futile. And so the rich and plastic descriptions of antique furniture, of old photographs, and of timeless streets are usually undermined by a word or phrase suggesting that their solidity and apparent timelessness are merely illusory. For example, the old daguerreotypes in "Sala vacía" ("Empty Hall") are deceiving by "their false nearness" ("su falsa cercanía"), and under close examination they "slip away/like useless dates/of blurred anniversaries" ("se escurren/como fechas inútiles/de aniversarios borrosos").[29] Another possible way of deceiving oneself about time, of "refuting" time, as Borges will later say, is found in the realm of ritualistic activity. The point is well exemplified in "El truco" ("The Trick"), a poem whose thematic material is a card game, but whose message is that in playing games—essentially a ritual—"normal" time is displaced. He writes, "At the edges of the card table/ordinary life is halted" ("En los lindes de la mesa/el vivir común se detiene").[30] By contrast, within the confines of the table—a magical zone—an ancient, timeless struggle is again waged, and the "players in their present ardor/copy the tricks of a remote age" ("los jugadores en fervor presente/copian remotas bazas").[31] Borges concludes the poem with the thought that this kind of activity "just barely" immortalizes the dead comrades whose struggles are relived. For a brief moment in the heat of the game, past and present are fused. The mythical kings, queens, and princes whose faces decorate the "cardboard amulets" become comrades-in-arms of the twentieth-century *criollos* seated about the table.

Borges' attempt to refute time, like his half-serious efforts to make reality more manageable through Berkeley's idealism, poses similar problems of interpretation. To what extent were these concerns an affective reaction to his return to changed childhood scenes and to what extent were they a product of his innate personality? To what extent were they early indications of an essential coldness which would lead him toward an increasingly "intellectual" literary manner? Was the Borges of 1923 a confident, if not cocky, young writer who deliberately wove into his poetry purely bookish reflections on time and space? Or was he a sensitive, insecure young man who sought escape from a dynamic and changing world by turning to philosophies which might help him deny the reality of time and of external objects? To reject one of these alternatives in favor of another would lead to an incomplete picture of the early Borges and to a distorted view of the mature writer. Surely the coolly intellectual player of literary games is apparent in the *Fervor;* but the warmer, more emotive, and more sincere poet is also there.

Borges' poetry, if it is examined with an eye unspoiled by reading the brittle geometrical narratives of his later years, reveals surprisingly sentimental, affectionate qualities. There are, for example, some touching love poems in *Fervor:* among these "Ausencia" ("Absence"), "Sábados" ("Saturdays"), and "Trofeo" ("Trophy") are especially noteworthy. And when Borges writes of his favorite streets, of patios and suburban gardens, he invokes a tone of filial devotion which suggests the warmest of personal relationships. He displays a mood of frankness and sincerity which those who know his work superficially do not usually associate with him. Indeed, some of the material in the first edition (omitted in later editions) is almost confessional in tone.[32] It seems as if the Borges of 1923 were at a crossroads. Had he been a man of different temperament, it is quite possible that he would have yielded to the temptation of creating literature of unrestrained personal catharsis. Instead, he chose to deny the emotive side of life in his art. At least he promised that he would do this in his poetry. As he writes in one of the last poems of the *Fervor:* "I must enclose my twilight tears/within the hard diamond of a poem./It matters not that one's soul may wander naked like the wind and alone . . ." ("He de encerrar el llanto de las tardes/en el duro diamante del poema./Nada importa que el alma/ande sola y desnuda como el viento . . .").[33]

II   Luna de enfrente (*Moon Across the Way*)

But Borges was not yet ready to sacrifice life and passion to art. Thus he states in his prologue to the collection that "Our daily existence is a dialogue of death and life. . . . There is a great deal of non-life in us, and chess, meetings, lectures, daily tasks are often mere representations of life, ways of being dead" ("Diálogo de muerte y vida es nuestro cotidiano vivir. . . . Mucha no vida hay en nosotros y el ajedrez, reuniones, conferencias, tareas, a veces son figuraciones de vida, maneras de estar muerto").[34] He states that he wished to avoid these "mere representations" of life in his poetry, that he would prefer to write of things which affect him emotionally, of "heavenly blue neighborhood garden-walls," for example. It is understandable, then, that among the twenty-eight compositions of *Luna de enfrente* poems of deep personal involvement should predominate over pieces of a more detached and more formalistic nature. A feeling of intimacy pervades the *Luna:* a third of the poems are in the second-person familiar form and the bulk of the remainder are in the first person. By contrast, the earlier *Fervor* contains only a few pieces directed to the familiar "you" (*tú*), while the majority are in the relatively impersonal third person. A further indication of the greater degree of intimacy of the *Luna de enfrente* is seen in Borges' tendency to personify such inanimate things as the Pampa, city streets, and the city itself. Finally, a substantial number of the compositions in the 1925 collection are love poems, among which are such memorable pieces as the "Antelación de amor" ("Anticipation of Love") and

the "Dualidá en una despedida" ("Duality on Saying Farewell").
Several typically Borgesian themes which appeared in *Fervor* are again seen in *Luna de enfrente*. The same tendency to soften or undermine exterior reality is evident in Borges' frequent use of the hazy light of twilight or dawn. This technique is well illustrated in such pieces as "Calle con almacén rosado" ("Street with a Pink Store"), "Dualidá en una despedida", "Montevideo," "Último sol en Villa Ortúzar" ("The Last Sun in Villa Ortuzar"), and others. Of even greater interest in the *Luna* is the poet's preoccupation with time. In this collection Borges' emphasis is on the relationship between time and memory rather than on the simple desire to halt time's flow. More precisely, memory becomes the *remanso*, the quiet backwater in which time's onward rush is checked. This relationship is very clear in "Montevideo," a poem in which Borges states that the more old-fashioned, less bustling Montevideo helps re-create the Buenos Aires of his early memories. Of the Uruguayan city he writes: "Like the memory of a frank friendship you are a clear and calm millpond in the twilight" ("Eres remansada y clara en la tarde como el recuerdo de una lisa amistad").[35] A somewhat similar verse appears in the magnificent "Antelación de amor," when the poet describes his beloved asleep as "calm and resplendent like a bit of happiness in memory's selection" ("quieta y resplandeciente como una dicha en la selección del recuerdo").[36] In these and in other poems memory performs the important function of preserving past experience against the onslaught of time. But, Borges implies, memory is also a storehouse, a kind of infinite filing cabinet, the contents of which we cannot always control. We may indeed remember too much. In "Los llanos" ("The Plains") he writes, "It is sad that memory includes everything/and especially if memories are unpleasant" ("Es triste que el recuerdo incluya todo/y más aún si es bochornoso el recuerdo").[37] Perhaps these lines prefigure Borges' bizarre account—to be written some twenty years later—of "Funes el memorioso," the man who remembered everything.

When Borges writes of time and memory in these poems he usually expresses strong personal feelings rather than philosophic detachment. The warmth typical of *Luna de enfrente* is especially clear in several of the love poems, among which "Antelación de amor" is the most impressive. The poet's message is simple and direct. Watching his beloved asleep, he feels that he sees a part of her denied even to herself; asleep she is out of the press of time, she is "calm and resplendent" like a pleasant and soothing thought summoned up from the storehouse of one's memory. Most important, in sleep she is absolved of time's ravages, she appears in her childlike essence, "as God is to see her with the fiction of time shattered" ("como Dios ha de verte,/desbaratada la ficción del Tiempo").[38] Much more might be said of "Antelación de amor": it is a superb poem in which Borges' often repressed lyricism appears clearly, though in fine balance with his characteristic intellectualism. In several other poems of the collection Borges combines the love theme with his underlying sensitivity to time. In the "Dualidá" he describes a scene of parting when "Inevitable time poured over the useless dike of an embrace" ("El tiempo inevitable redivulgaba sobre el inútil tajamar del abrazo").[39] Though less pronounced, the same conjunction of themes appears in "Casas como ángeles" ("Houses Like Angels") and "Mi vida entera" ("My Whole Life").

Some two years before Borges published *Luna de enfrente* he was asked to answer a series of questions for a magazine survey of young writers. In answer to a question about his age, he wrote "I have already wearied twenty-two years" ("Ya he cansado veintidós años").[40] The choice of words here is significant, for there is curious tone of the world-weary old man even in his work of the mid-twenties. This tone, contrasting markedly with the passionate lyricism of several pieces in the *Luna de enfrente*, takes the form of the poet's proclaiming that he has already lived a good deal of his life and that he will do nothing new in the future. The theme is very clear in "Mi vida entera": "I have crossed the sea./I have lived in many lands; I have seen one woman and two or three men/ . . . I have savored many words./I profoundly believe that this is all and that I will neither see nor do any new things" ("He atravesado el mar./He practicado muchas tierras; he visto una mujer y dos otros hombres./ . . . He paladeado numerosas palabras./Creo profundamente que eso es todo y que ni veré ni ejecutaré cosas nuevas").[41] A somewhat similar tone is evoked in some of the poems describing the pampa: in "Los llanos," for example, Borges tries to infuse the plains with a feeling of tiredness and resignation suggestive of his own mood. It is difficult to determine what lies behind this pose of bored world-weariness. Is Borges retreating from life or is he simply stating what has become a cornerstone of his esthetic edifice: that there is nothing new under the sun; that changes, progress, novelty, and history are simply a reshuffling of a limited number of pre-existing elements? Perhaps this is the philosophy which he intends to set forth in the cryptic line which ends his poem "Manuscrito hallado en un libro de Joseph Conrad" ("Manuscript Found in a Book by Joseph Conrad"): "River, the first river. Man, the first man" ("El río, el primer río. El hombre, el primer hombre").[42]

While history may be nothing more than the recurrence or the reshuffling of what has always been, Borges is nonetheless fascinated by historical events and personalities. Several of the pieces in the *Luna* show this interest. The dramatic death of the nineteenth-century gaucho leader Quiroga is very effectively commemorated in "El General Quiroga va en coche al muere" ("General Quiroga Rides to His Death by Coach"); the death of his own ancestor, Colonel Francisco Borges provides the subject matter of another piece; and "Dulcia linquimus arva" ("We Gently Abandon Our Fields") evokes the early days of settlement on the Pampa. Of the three, the poem to Quiroga is the most interesting for several reasons. For one, the night scene of Quiroga's coach rocking across the moonlit Pampa has a dramatic, almost romantic feeling of movement, uncommon in much of Borges' poetry. Secondly, though he was still more or less faithful to the free verse tenets of his youth, Borges saw fit to place the poem within a fairly regular structure—rhythmic lines of about fourteen syllables arranged in quatrains having considerable assonance. The effect of this form is striking; it suggests the beat of the horses' hooves and the rocking of the coach racing on toward its encounter with destiny:

> The coach swayed back and forth rumbling the
> hills:
> An emphatic, enormous funeral galley.
> Four death-black horses in the darkness
> Pulled six fearful and one watchful brave man
>
> . . . .
> That sly, trouble-making Córdoba rabble
> (thought Quiroga), what power have they over me?

Here am I firm in the stirrup of life
Like a stake driven deep in the heart of the
pampa . . .

(El coche se hamacaba rezongando la altura:
un galerón enfático, enorme, funerario.
Cuatro tapaos con pinta de muerte en la negrura
tironeaban seis miedos y un valor desvelado.

. . . .
Esa cordobesada bochinchera y ladina
(meditaba Quiroga) ¿qué ha de poder con mi alma?
Aquí estoy afianzado y metido en la vida
como la estaca pampa bien metida en la pampa . . .)[43]

It is to Borges' credit as a poet that despite his mild adherence to
the restrictive poetic tenets of *Ultraísmo* he sensed the rightness
of a more traditional form for this particular poem.

In "El General Quiroga va en coche al muere" Borges provides
an insight into the kind of historical characters and events which
were to dominate much of his later work, especially his prose.
What fascinates him are those moments in which an individual—
soldier, bandit, or similar man of action—reaches a crucial point in
his life: the dramatic junctures where a turn of fate, a sudden decision, or a dazzling revelation cause a man to follow one path or
another. Such events are delicate points of balance which determine whether a man shall become a hero or traitor, a martyr or
coward. Borges is especially intrigued by them since they often
provide a glimpse of an alternative track for history. What would
have been the course of Argentine history if Rosas had not killed
Facundo or if (as in one of his very recent poems) King Charles
of England had not been beheaded? "El General Quiroga va en
coche al muere" is also significant in that it reveals another important side of Borges' interests. Though he may be a shy and retiring
bibliophile, he does have an undeniable affection for men of action: gunmen, pirates, *compadres* (a kind of Buenos Aires neighborhood tough), ancient warriors, and modern spies fill the pages
of his poetry, essays, and fiction.

To conclude, *Luna de enfrente* is a collection of poems in which
Borges reveals many of his intellectual preoccupations but even
more of his affective life. The love theme and a confessional
tone figure prominently in a substantial number of the poems;

they are even more pronounced in some of the pieces published in the original collection of 1925, but omitted from later editions.[44] The typically Borgesian treatment of external reality and time is also very evident in these poems, especially in those pieces dealing with memory. His interest in history—first seen in his poem to Rosas in *Fervor*—continues to grow. Finally Borges introduces in *Luna* a mood that has come to occupy an important place in much of his work: that of the man who has apparently done and seen everything and seems convinced that novelty is mere illusion.

As an example of poetic art, the *Luna de enfrente* is a rather uneven collection, especially if it is judged by the complete first edition. Borges' fine metaphors and striking adjectives, however, serve to make a number of the poems exceptionally beautiful. The high point of the collection, in the writer's view, is the finely wrought "Antelación de amor." Aside from the inherent lyricism of the piece, it is an example of how structural excellence can enhance total poetic impact, even when the poet is working in a completely free verse form. Among the pieces of comparable quality is the "Dualidá en una despedida," a fine love poem containing a striking simile in which the poet compares his steadily growing affection to the Judaic Hanukkah candelabra whose warm glow increases with the passing of each day. Though it may lack the lyrical intensity of Borges' love poetry, "El General Quiroga va en coche al muere" must also be placed among the best poems in the collection by dint of its rhythmic flow and romantic rendering of a dramatic event in Argentine history.

III Cuaderno San Martín (*San Martín Notebook*)

The last group of poems Borges chose to publish as a collection, *Cuaderno San Martín* (1929), contains only twelve pieces, one of which, "Arrabal en que pesa el campo" ("Suburb in Which the Country Lies Heavily"), has been omitted from more recent editions. Two themes dominate these poems: nostalgia for the past, and death. Often the two blend in a mood of elegiac evocation. Thus in the most memorable poems of the book Borges writes of the "mythical" founding of Buenos Aires; of his beloved Palermo district as it was at the close of the nineteenth century; of his grandfather Isidoro Acevedo; of the final resting place of ancestors, the Recoleta Cemetery; and of the suicide of his friend and fellow poet Francisco López Merino.

What the poet preserves in his memory in a sense lives; only what is gone *and* forgotten is really dead. In "Elegía de los portones" ("Elegy to Gates"), for example, Borges describes the act of forgetting as "a minuscule death" ("una muerte chica").[45] Yet he is perfectly aware that death—real death—is undeniable: he knows that his attempts to negate its reality through memory and through poetry will be frustrated. He is haunted by the song of the wandering slum-minstrel in the poem to the Chacarita Cemetery, "Death is life already lived./Life is approaching death." ("La muerte es vida vivida,/la vida es muerte que viene"). It even haunts him when he writes, in the same piece, that he doesn't believe in the cemetery's decrepitude and that "the fullness of only one rose is greater than all your tombstones" ("la plenitud de una sola rosa es más que tus marmoles").[46]

But the poems dedicated to Buenos Aires cemeteries, with their restrained elegiac tone, seem to pale by comparison with the deeply moving tribute to López Merino. Here Borges faces not death's mystery or horror but the brutal fact that López deliberately chose to "refuse all the world's tomorrows" ("rehusar todas las mañanas del mundo"). The poet realizes the utter uselessness of trying to undo what has already been done. He can "only speak of the dishonor of roses that were powerless to restrain . . ./and of the opprobium of the day that allowed the bullet and the end" ("Sólo nos queda entonces/decir el deshonor de las rosas que no supieron demorarte,/el oprobio del día que te permitió el balazo y el fin.") All that Borges is left with is the hope that perhaps each person shapes his own hereafter and that death will be like a favorite dream in which all the unpleasantness of the world will be forgotten. If this is true, he tells his dead friend, "Your death is a light and delicate thing/like the verse in which you are forever waiting for us" ("entonces es ligera tu muerte,/como los versos en que siempre estás esperándonos"). Aside from expressing a deep sense of personal loss Borges is shocked and dismayed that López would voluntarily give up all that life has to offer. While the opprobium of living may be very real, there is much that makes existence worthwhile. In a series of beautifully turned and revealing lines Borges describes these treasures which his friend has rejected: "the intimate, undecipherable news items that music tells us/the homeland which gives us fig trees and cisterns/the passionate force of love that justifies the soul/those charged moments/by virtue of which the honor of reality is saved" ("las íntimas, indescifrables noticias que nos cuenta la música,/la patria que condesciende a higuera y aljibe,/la ardiente gravitación del amor que justifica el alma/los cargados minutos/por los que se salva el honor de la realidad").[47]

The poem to López Merino may well be the finest piece in the collection: certainly it is one of the most deeply felt and one of the most sincere Borges has ever written. There are, however, other notable poems in the *Cuaderno San Martín*, such as the pieces dedicated to the two great cemeteries of Buenos Aires, the poor man's Chacarita, where "death is colorless, hollow, numerical;/ and is reduced to names and dates" ("la muerte es incolora, hueca, numérica;/se disminuye a fechas y nombres"),[48] and the cemetery of the upper and middle classes, the Recoleta, where death is dignified and "proper." Impressive too are the nostalgic poems in which he writes of his "dark loyalty" ("lealtad oscura") to the *barrio*, "Elegía de los portones" and "Barrio norte" ("North Side").

One of the most interesting pieces in the collection is on the death of Borges' ancestor, Isidoro Acevedo. Aside from its intrinsic value, this poem is noteworthy because in it Borges gives a clear hint of the kind of literature he would produce in the decade to follow. This "prefiguring"—to use one of his own favorite terms —of his future prose occurs in the description of Acevedo's last day. The old man lying on his deathbed in a state of feverish delirium plans a complete military compaign in his mind. Though Acevedo only mutters a few fragmentary phrases, Borges uses these as a point of departure to re-create a very concrete fantasy which he assumes his moribund grandfather was in effect experiencing:

He dreamt of two armies/which were going into the shadows of battle;/he enumerated each commanding officer, the banners, each unit/. . . He surveyed the pampa/noted the rough country that the infantry might seize/and the smooth plain in which a cavalry strike would be invincible./He made a final survey,/he gathered together the thousands of faces that a man unknowingly knows after many years:/ bearded faces that are probably fading away in daguerreotypes,/faces that lived near his own in Puente Alsina and Cepeda./. . . He gathered an army of Buenos Aires' ghosts . . ./. . . He died in the military service of his faith in the *patria*.

(Soñó con dos ejércitos/que entraban en la sombra de una batalla;/ enumeró los comandos, las banderas, las unidades./ . . . . . . Hizo leva de pampa:/vió terreno quebrado para que pudiera aferrarse la infantería/y llanura resuelta para que el tirón de la caballería fuera invencible./Hizo una leva última,/congregó los miles de rostros que el hombre sabe sin saber después de los años:/caras de barba que se estarán desvaneciendo en daguerrotipos,/caras que vivieron junto a la suya en el Puente Alsina y Cepeda./ . . . . . . juntó un ejército de sombras porteñas/. . . murió en milicia de su convicción por la patria.)[49]

Those who are familiar with Borges' fiction may appreciate the similarity of this poem to short stories such as the "Ruinas circulares" ("The Circular Ruins"): there are only a few steps between describing the disturbing concreteness of dreams and suggesting that what we call the real world may actually be the product of some unknown being's dream.

IV   Later Poems

Borges continued to write poetry after 1929, though his output of verse, particularly during the 1930's and 1940's, was not very great. There may be some significance to the fact that between the summer of 1929 and the spring of 1931 he published nothing. This hiatus may have been due to the extremely unsettled political and economic conditions of this period: a similar pattern can be observed in the literary activity of other Argentine writers during the same two years. When Borges resumed publishing, he devoted himself chiefly to essays and literary criticism, genres in which he had been working steadily throughout the 1920's. It was not until 1934 that he again began writing poetry; oddly enough he broke his poetic silence with two pieces composed in English. These were followed by "Insomnio" (1936), "La noche cíclica" ("The Cyclical Night," 1940), "Del infierno y del cielo" ("Of Heaven and Hell," 1942), "Poema conjectural" ("A Conjectural Poem," 1943), and "Poema del cuarto elemento" ("Poem of the Fourth Element," 1944). Between March, 1944 and April, 1953 Borges wrote no poetry, at least he published none, yet it was during this period that he produced his most celebrated stories and a number of important essays. The middle 1950's to the present (1968) has seen Borges' return to his first love, poetry. Late in 1960 he published *El hacedor* (*Dreamtigers*), a volume which contains twenty-four poems along with a number of short prose pieces. Since then he has published poetry almost exclusively: these compositions, though few in number, have apppeared with some regularity in Buenos Aires' leading daily, *La Nación*.

The seven poems which Borges wrote between 1934 and 1944 are, at first glance, quite dissimilar in both form and content. The "Two English Poems," for example, are amorous in theme and are cast in extremely free verse, so much so that they could be regarded as prose poems:

> I offer you my ancestors, my dead men; the ghosts that living men have honoured in marble: my father's father killed in the frontier of Buenos Aires, two bullets through his lungs, bearded and dead, wrapped by his soldiers in the hide of a cow; my mother's grandfather—just twenty-four—heading a charge of three hundred men in Perú, now ghosts on vanished horses.[50]

"Insomnio" is also written in free verse, but unlike the "Two English Poems" its lines are generally shorter and its appearance on the printed page is more traditional. "La noche cíclica," in sharp contrast to most of the poetry Borges had published previously, is written in neat quatrains rhymed in the *cuarteto* pattern (*abba*). In the next two poems of this group "Del infierno y del cielo" and "Poema conjetural," Borges reverted to a rather free unrhymed form, only to use the *cuarteto* again in 1944 in his "Poema del cuarto elemento." The significance of these formal shifts should not be overestimated: they only indicate that Borges would from this point on, be bounded neither by the orthodoxy of his free-verse *Ultraísta* years nor by the orthodoxy of traditional forms.

Why Borges chose to write the "Two English Poems" in the language of his paternal grandmother is a matter which neither he nor his commentators have discussed. Perhaps these compositions merely represent a tour de force or perhaps they indicate a feeling of alienation from the not too pleasant surroundings of Buenos Aires of the early 1930's. Certain details in the poems suggest the latter possibility. Borges reveals an ennui and desperation in these pieces which are clearly lacking in the earlier poetry. The opening lines of the first poem are indicative of this mood: "The useless dawn finds me in a deserted street corner. . . ." A bit later he speaks of the night as having left him "some hated friends to

chat/with, music for dreams, and the smoking of/bitter ashes.
The things that my hungry heart/has no use for." The piece ends
on a note of great intensity summed up in some of Borges' finest
lines. At daybreak, the poet says, "The shattering dawn finds me
in a deserted street of my city." The "lazily and incessantly beautiful" woman to whom the poem is addressed is gone. The poet is
left with only memories of the encounter and with a desperate
longing: "I must get at you, somehow: I put away those/illustri-
ous toys you have left me, I want your hidden look, your real
smile—that lonely,/mocking smile your cool mirror knows." [51] The
same tone of desperation pervades the second English poem when
the poet asks his beloved, "What can I hold you with?/I offer you
lean streets, desperate sunsets, the/moon of jagged suburbs./I
offer you the bitterness of a man who has looked/long and long at
the lonely moon." Throughout the remainder of the piece—as
quotable as any Borges has written—he continues to enumerate
what he can "offer." The last lines reinforce and climax the entire
poem: "I can give you my loneliness, my darkness, the/hunger of
my heart; I am trying to bribe you/with uncertainty, with danger,
with defeat." [52] The details of these poems give a picture of almost
surrealistic disintegration: *lean* streets, *shattering* dawn, *jagged*
suburbs. These are not typically Borgesian adjectives. And in "Insomnio," a poem whose intent is admittedly quite different from
that of the English pieces, the poet's restlessness is aggravated by
visions of "shattered tenements" ("despedazado arrabal") of
"leagues of obscene garbage-strewn pampa" ("leguas de pampa
basurera y obscena"),[53] and similar scenes.

The references to insomnia, to loneliness, to bitterness, and the
use of adjectives suggestive of disintegration have little in common with the often ardent, though seldom desperate, poems of
the earlier collections. The unusual character of his verse of the
1930's points to the fact that he was undergoing a period of transition in his literary career. Borges seems, moreover, to have
suffered some kind of personal crisis, aggravated, perhaps, by a
political and economic environment distasteful to him. An examination of his prose of the mid-1930's supports this view. It is especially significant that the genesis of his distinctive fantasy fiction—
a literature of escape, many would say—comes precisely at this
time.

The four remaining poems of the decade 1934–44 reflect a number of the themes which were then coming to dominate Borges' prose. These compositions lack the mood of desperation of the English poems and of "Insomnio": rather, they seem cold and overly intellectual. In "La noche cíclica" (1940), a philosophical piece on the idea of cyclical history, Borges makes rather bookish references to Hume, Pythagoras, and Anaxagoras. The poem's theme, given in the first lines, "The arduous students of Pythagoras discovered it:/Stars and men return cyclically" ("Lo supieron los arduous alumnos de Pitágoras:/Los astros y los hombres vuelven cíclicamente") crops up again in the very last line when the poet remarks "Constant eternity again returns to my human flesh/and the memory—or the project?—of an incessant poem:/'The arduous students of Pythagoras discovered it . . .'" ("Vuelve a mi carne humana la eternidad constante/Y el recuerdo¿ el proyecto? de un poema incesante:/'Lo supieron los arduos alumnos de Pitágoras . . .'").[54] The implication, of course, is that the poem will begin again and continue repeating itself ad infinitum.

In "Del infierno y del cielo" (1942) Borges states that instead of the traditional kind of Heaven and Hell, we may encounter in the hereafter an enigmatic eternal face which would be "for the reprobates, Hell;/for the chosen, Heaven" ("Será para los réprobos, Infierno;/para los elegidos, Paraíso").[55] The idea of encountering a face which may be one's own suggests Borges' growing cultivation of the *otredad* theme in his prose. Significantly, the poems of this period are, in the 1964 edition of his poetry, grouped under the heading "El otro, el mismo" ("The other man, himself"). This theme of dual existence was to be superbly expressed some years later in his well-known parable, "Borges y yo" ("Borges and I").

The "Poema conjetural" (1943) represents on the one hand a return to an earlier poetic style, and on the other the incorporation of thematic material more typical of Borges' prose. The composition, one of Borges' own favorites, was once chosen by him as the synthesis of all his poetry.[56] The poem describes the death of an ancestor, Francisco Laprida, shot by the gaucho leader Aldao during the early nineteenth century. Laprida's dramatic recognition of the fact that he was about to die gives the piece its impact and echoes the theme of "El General Quiroga va en coche al

muere." Laprida experiences a kind of "secret jubilation" when he
realizes that his death, under this particular conjunction of circumstances is his unique destiny:

> At last I have found
> my destiny as a South American.
> The multiple labyrinth of steps
> that my days have woven since one day in my childhood
> Has brought me to this miserable afternoon
> At last I have discovered
> the hidden key to my life
> The fate of Francisco de Laprida
> the missing letter, the completed form
> that God knew since the beginning.
> In the mirror of this night I attain
> my unsuspected eternal face.

> (Al fin me encuentro
> con mi destino sudamericano.
> A esta ruinosa tarde me llevaba
> el laberinto múltiple de pasos
> que mis días tejieron desde un día
> de la niñez. Al fin he descubierto
> la recóndita clave de mis años,
> la suerte de Francisco de Laprida,
> la letra que faltaba, la perfecta
> forma que supo Dios desde el principio.
> En el espejo de esta noche alcanzo
> mi insospechado rostro eterno.) [57]

The idea of the "hidden key" to a problem, the familiar labyrinthine view of the world, and the theme of an all-knowing divinity
who seems only slightly concerned with man's attempts to solve
eternal riddles, are, of course, notions which figure prominently in
much of Borges' prose.

The most recent phase of Borges' poetry begins in 1953 and
continues to the present. Were it not for the fact that prose fiction
has a much broader general appeal, and that it translates much
more readily than verse, Borges might well have been considered
primarily a poet. As it is, many of his ardent admirers, especially
foreigners, are hardly aware of this aspect of his work. Yet those
who know him well have often remarked that he would like to be

thought of as a poet.[58] His dedication to poetry in the waning years of his life is a good indication of the high regard in which he holds this genre. Moreover, the awareness of not having realized his full lyric potential acts as a goad, as it does for all serious poets. This very point is the theme of his "Mateo XXV, 30" ("Matthew XXV, 30," 1953), in which he likens himself to the foolish virgins in the parable of the ten talents. Though he has been given everything, all the raw material a poet might desire, "stars, bread, oriental and occidental libraries/ . . . a human body to walk the earth/ . . . Algebra and fire . . ." ("Estrellas, pan, bibliotecas orientales y occidentales/ . . . un cuerpo humano para andar por la tierra/ . . . Algebra y fuego . . ."), a voice tells him that "you have wasted the years and they have wasted you,/and you have still not written the poem" ("Has gastado los años y te han gastado,/y todavía no has escrito el poema").[59]

A few generalizations may be made regarding the poetry of the last ten years. One of these is that Borges, except for a very few compositions, has now chosen to cast his verse in traditionally rhymed and metered forms. He has explained his choice on the basis of his blindness, claiming that rhyme makes it easier for him to compose without reference to the written word. At any rate, his favorite vehicles seem to be the sonnet (in both the English and Italianate form) and the *cuarteto* which he had used earlier in the "Noche cíclica."

To generalize about the content of the recent poems is more difficult. Certainly history, viewed at times in the microcosm of a small but crucial event, and at other times in broad sweep, remains a major preoccupation. Closely related to his interest in the specifics of history is the constant fascination with time. And perhaps at the very root of all these concerns is a notion which has an almost obsessive recurrence in Borges' poetry as well as in his prose: the idea of the world as a complex enigma, expressed in the form of the labyrinth, or as the dream-made-real of a capricious creator. These are the underlying themes of his recent poetry, though on the surface Borges' subject matter reflects his current interests and activities: a half-dozen pieces deal with various aspects of ancient Germanic and Anglo-Saxon culture; several poems show his continuing fascination with his family's history; another group deals with certain facets of Jewish tradition; several touch upon great moments in England's past; and a few attest to Borges' unending infatuation with Buenos Aires and its way of life.

A number of these later poems reveal a sharpened self-consciousness: a kind of looking at oneself from the "outside" or as in a mirror. This theme of "otherness" (or *otredad* in Spanish) has already been mentioned in connection with this composition of 1943, the "Poema conjectural." A similar expression of *otredad* characterizes a poem of the *Hacedor* group, "Los espejos" ("Mirrors"). In this piece the poet confesses an inexplicable childish horror at the thought of "the other" who looks back at him from mirrors or similar reflecting surfaces. A further development of the theme is seen in the first poem of the same collection, "Poema de los dones" ("Poem of the Gifts"), where Borges describes his wanderings though the National Library. He thinks of others who have done exactly the same thing: "On wandering through these slow galleries/I usually sense, with a vague and holy chill/That I am the other one, the one who's dead, who has probably taken/these same steps on the same days/Which of the two is writing this poem? . . ." ("Al errar por las lentas galerías/Suelo sentir con vago horror sagrado/Que soy el otro, el muerto, que habrá dado/Los mismos pasos en los mismos días./¿Cuál de los dos escribe este poema . . . ?")[60] The "other" to whom Borges refers can be interpreted in several ways. It may be an earlier director of the library (Paul Groussac who served in this capacity when Borges was a child and to whom he refers in the poem), or it may be Borges himself—viewed as a kind of biographical datum, rather than as the simple expression of one man's consciousness at a specific time and place. Another possible interpretation stems from an idea frequently expressed in Borges' prose: that all men are each other, that when doing *exactly* what another person has done we are, in some sense, that person. But the "Poema de los dones" is memorable for other reasons. The poem expresses, with considerable irony and resignation, Borges' feelings on being finally given the post he had for many years desired, that of director of the National Library, only to have this event coincide with his becoming almost totally blind. In the limpid first stanza he writes, "Let no one cheapen by tears or reproach/This declaration of the skill/of God, who, with magnificent irony/Gave me, at one stroke, books and the night" ("Nadie rebaje a lágrima o reproche/Esta declaración de la maestría/De Dios, que con magnífica ironía/Me dio a la vez los libros y la noche").[61]

The second "Poema de los dones," written several years after the *Hacedor* poems, and one of the most recent of Borges' major poems, is truer to its title than is the earlier piece. Borges, now in his sixties, feels that the time to recount his "gifts" is at hand: hence this unusual poem in which he does little more than list all those things which he values. Yet the piece is very effective—aside from its value as a catalogue of Borges' world. He directs his thanks to "The divine Labyrinth of causes and effects" ("al divino/Laberinto de los efectos y de las causas") for some seventy-five specific items. These range from the face of Helen of Troy to the overthrow of Perón; from the "stripes of the tiger" to Zeno's Tortoise; from Socrates' last day to a "morning in Texas"; from a Viking epitaph to Verlaine, "as innocent as a bird." Chess, Schopenhauer, the *Thousand and One Nights,* the *patria,* bravery, bread, salt, and friendship, all are duly listed and appreciated. Near the end of the piece he expresses an idea which is closely related to his basic theory of literary art and to his view of reality. He gives thanks for Whitman and St. Francis "who have already written the poem" ("que ya escribieron el poema"), after which he states that "the poem is inexhaustible/and it becomes confused with the sum of beings/and it will never get to the final verse/And it varies as do men" ("el poema es inagotable/y se confunde con la suma de las criaturas/Y no llegará jamás al último verso/Y varía según los hombres").[62] What can we say about the precise meaning of "the poem" in this context? Borges is perhaps asserting that all literature is essentially one literature; that all writers—perhaps all cultures—shape it, give to it and draw from it. He very likely believes that "the poem"—the literary rendering of reality—thus cannot be original; that like the world itself it is a periodic rearrangement of a finite number of elements. The final lines of the second "Poema de los dones" are less enigmatic: they are the gentle and resigned expression of a poet who knows well that twilight is at hand: "I give thanks for sleep and death,/Those two unrevealed treasures/For the intimate gifts I have not enumerated/For music, that mysterious form of time" ("Por el sueño y la muerte,/Esos dos tesoros ocultos,/Por los íntimos dones que no enumero,/Por la música, misteriosa forma del tiempo").[63]

Despite his blindness and despite the autumnal mood suggested above, Borges' poetic production of the last several years has been indeed rich. In addition to the poems already discussed, his recent poems include many of his finest pieces: for example, the lyrical evocation of his father's voice in "La lluvia" ("Rain"); or the moving poem on the faith of the nameless criminal crucified beside Christ in "Lucas XIII." Though many of his essential themes recur, Borges' work still shows much lyrical power. "Elegía" (1963), a poem in which he recounts his experiences and travels of recent years, takes a charming amorous turn at the end; he sadly confesses that after all is said and done he really hasn't seen anything "except the face of a Buenos Aires girl,/a face that doesn't wish to be remembered" ("Sino el rostro de una muchacha de Buenos Aires,/un rostro que no quiere que lo recuerde").[64] A piece written as late as 1967 on the death of England's Charles I attests his perpetual fascination with crucial moments in history. In short, in his late sixties Borges remained an active poet.

Poetry, it must be remembered, has always been an essential activity for Borges. Even during the years of little poetic activity, he felt the genre's primacy in his scale of literary values. His comments of 1952 in this regard are significant: "I understood that poetry was forbidden to me except in flashes, and in flashes lost in my works. . . . I think that with the stories I write, and with the essays too, I give as much poetry as I can . . ." ("Yo comprendí que la poesía me estaba vedada salvo por ráfagas perdidas en las obras . . . creo que con los cuentos que escribo, creo que con los artículos también, doy lo que puedo dar de poesía que no es mucho . . .").[65] In short, the desire to incorporate poetic feeling into all his literary expression has always characterized Borges' work. Poetry has been, and rightfully so, the most personal of his genres and the one to which he constantly returns. Present in everything about us, it has for Borges a humble and everyday quality. It is in this sense that the lovely sixth stanza of his "Arte poética" is best appreciated: "They tell how Ulysses, glutted with wonders,/Wept with love to descry his Ithaca/Humble and green. Art is that Ithaca/Of green eternity, not of wonders" ("Cuentan que Ulises, harto de prodigios,/Lloró de amor al divisar su Itaca/Verde y humilde. El arte es esa Itaca/De verde eternidad, no de prodigios").[66]

CHAPTER 3

Borges the Essayist

BORGES began writing essays and literary criticism at almost the same time that he began writing poetry. It is not surprising, then, that his early essays often reflect the preoccupations of a poet: comments on fellow poets, the nature of imagery, and the characteristics of the poetic movement to which he subscribed. Yet other interests, aside from purely literary ones, appear in these early collections. His first book of essays, *Inquisiciones* (1925), contains at least two pieces dealing with philosophic questions, while in the second collection, *Tamaño de mi esperanza* (1926), he analyzes *criollismo*—the problem of defining a distinctive Argentine cultural identity—in its nonliterary as well as in its literary manifestations. The essays of *El idioma de los argentinos* (*The Language of the Argentines,* 1928) and *Evaristo Carriego* (1930) in the main follow the trajectory outlined in his work of the early 1920's in that they emphasize literary studies and a further probe of the *criollismo* problem. Parallels with his poetry of the period are also very much in evidence: neighborhood scenes, the tango, and similar picturesque aspects of Buenos Aires life figure prominently in both genres.

Borges' fifth collection of essays, *Discusión,* appearing in 1932, marks a new emphasis in his essayistic work. Certain philosophic concerns, especially his fascination with space, time, and unusual cosmologies, which had appeared occasionally in his prose and which underlay much of his verse, now come to the surface in well-developed essays. It would be incorrect to say that Borges changes his essayistic style at this point in his career, as it would be misleading to claim that the ideas in *Discusión* are essentially different from those he had expressed earlier. Rather he begins to shift his focal point away from Buenos Aires life—the *barrio,* local bards and heroes—to foreign literatures, particularly those of non-Hispanic cultures, and to philosophic concerns. That the early

56

1930's may be considered a period of crisis and reorientation in
Borges' literary development is confirmed by studying the essays
of these troubled years. One piece in particular, an unusually bit-
ter critique of his nation and of his city, "Nuestras imposibilidades" ("Our Impossibilities") (included in the 1932 edition of
Discusión but written in 1931), gives further evidence to support
the idea that the external realities of the period had a very considerable impact upon Borges' internalized literary world. *Discusión*
sets the course for many of the essays to follow. Furthermore
many of its themes are the same ones which shape Borges' prose
fiction, as yet in the mind of their author rather than on paper.

Following *Discusión,* Borges' rich essayistic production provides thorny problems for the bibliographer, as well as for those
who are interested in the ideas themselves. It must be remembered that the bulk of the essays, articles, reviews, and literary
notes which may be considered under the general category of essayistic writings first appeared individually in various magazines
and newspapers. With regard to the early collections the dates of
originals and the dates of the collective publication are quite
close, but in the more recent books of essays this is not always the
case.[1] Further complications arise from the fact that the same
piece may appear in two different collections; and that second
editions often contain additions to and deletions from the originals. At any rate, the sixth collection of essays, *Historia de la eternidad* (1936), includes pieces covering the period 1932–36, while
Otras inquisiciones (1952) presents selected essays representative
of some fifteen years' work (1937–52). Between the publication of
these collections, two important essays appeared separately as individual publications: the rather philosophical *Nueva refutación
del tiempo* (*A New Refutation of Time,* 1947), and the more literary *Aspectos de la literatura gauchesca* (1950). Beginning in
1953, second editions of some of the essay collections have appeared as part of the Emecé publishing house's project of editing
Borges' complete works;[2] but with the exception of the short
prose compositions of *El hacedor*—assuming that these may be
called essays—Borges' activity in this genre has declined sharply
during the 1960's.

In assessing Borges' total production of nonfictional prose one
should not lose sight of the great range covered by his writing and
of the fact that a great deal of his more popular work has never

been reprinted in his essay collections. For every one of his well-known, sophisticated, and highly intellectualized essays, he has written many unpretentious and informative book reviews. During the late 1930's, for example, his column "Libros y autores extranjeros" ("Foreign Books and Authors") (in the popular magazine, *Hogar*) gave the average Argentine reader an appetizing taste of many relatively unknown literary delights. His work as a reviewer for such publications as *Sur* and the *Anales de Buenos Aires* during the 1940's was also noteworthy. Nor should Borges' contributions as a prologuist and editor be overlooked in surveying his nonfictional prose. His anthologies of fantastic fiction (done in collaboration with Silvina Ocampo and Bioy Casares) and of detective stories (in collaboration with Bioy Casares) were widely circulated. Borges wrote introductions and prologues for dozens of books, many of them translations of such celebrated American authors as William Faulkner, Henry James, and Bret Harte. He also collaborated in the preparation of several anthologies of Argentine literature and, in 1951, wrote (with Delia Ingenieros) a guide to *Antiguas literaturas germánicas*. These far-ranging writings, while not of primary interest in our analysis of Borges' literary trajectory, do help refute the charges which have occasionally been made that he is an intellectual snob, and strictly "A writer's writer." Borges may well be an extremely bookish person, but he nonetheless wishes to share the adventure, excitement, and pleasures of good reading with a large audience. In short, when his total activity is weighed, his role as a literary divulgator and mentor must be taken into consideration.

Borges made his debut as an essayist in one of the leading literary magazines of the 1920's, *Nosotros*. His first piece, "Ultraísmo" (December, 1921), is an explanation and defense of the poetic movement to which he had become attracted in Spain and which he later imported to Buenos Aires. In it he says that the young poets of his generation feel that thematic materials and techniques of the *rubendarianos* (followers of the leading Modernist poet, Rubén Darío) have been completely exhausted and that a new esthetic theory is needed. *Ultraísmo*, he states, is one of the possible courses for poetry to take. The principal tenets of the movement have already been noted in an earlier chapter.[3] That these principles are not nearly as radical as their author would

have us believe bears repeating, as does the fact that Borges soon
abandoned them. It may also be significant that he chose not to
include this item in any of his essay collections. To date
"Ultraísmo" has appeared in print only in the yellowing pages of
Nosotros and in the text of scholarly studies of Borges' early work.

I Inquisiciones

Borges' ideas on poetic theory—and by extension on language
itself—dominate the essays collected in *Inquisiciones*. With the exception of two philosophical pieces (of which more later), all deal
with specific writers, literary *criollismo*, the function of metaphor,
and the like. Much of the *Ultraísta* spirit is reflected in these essays: in "Ejecución de tres palabras" ("The Execution of Three
Words"), for example, he attacks some of the specific literary sins
of the followers of Darío by calling for the obliteration of "ineffable," "mysterious," and "blue" from the poetic lexicon.[4] In his
piece on Herrera y Reissig, he criticizes the Uruguayan Modernist
for his unfounded and blind faith in the connotative power of
words.[5] In "Después de las imágenes" ("After the Images") he
takes his own generation of Argentine poets to task for not producing any really substantial verse and especially for their juvenile experimentation with metaphor.[6] Yet Borges does not confine
himself to negative cricitism; several of the pieces in this collection reveal the positive side of his literary values. Thus in the
"Menoscabo y grandeza de Quevedo" ("Discredit and Grandeur
of Quevedo") he analyzes the great Spanish prosist's sensitivity to
"the problematical nature of language" ("lo problemático del
lenguaje"). Borges appears to be fascinated with much in
Quevedo's style. He singles out his penchant for mixing high-
sounding, cultured terms with plebeian words which nonetheless
carry exactly the same ideas as their illustrious bretheren. This
technique, Borges notes, gives an effect of freshness, of intense
reality to the Spaniard's writing: one which makes his readers see
the world "as if for the first time" ("por vez primera al espíritu").
Borges states that he admires Quevedo's intellectualism, but he
does note that it can be "inept." Far from being a blind devotee of
his predecessor, he qualifies his admiration by remarking that
Quevedo was more "intense" than "original." [7]

Borges uses several other essays of the collection as points of
departure for further analysis of metaphor and poetic language.

In his highly laudatory piece on Sir Thomas Browne, for example, he notes with approval the Englishman's penchant for Latinisms and for using words in the sense of their Classical etymology. Borges goes on to explain that many words, in the Romance as well as Germanic languages, have multiple meanings: those which have grown through centuries of regional development, and the meanings which still conserve their original Latin connotation.[8] While these ideas are hardly those of a sophisticated linguist, they do help clarify one of the techniques Borges frequently employs in his verse: the use of common words in the sense of their classical roots. We also see, on the linguistic level, another expression of Borges' characteristic desire to freeze time and to negate the flow of historical change. In the "Examen de metáforas" (*"An Examination of Metaphors"*) Borges sheds more light on his own poetic techniques. For example, he notes his fondness for images which express temporal values in spatial terms: as in illustration he shows how the length of the princesses' braided hair (in one of his favorite books, the *Thousand and One Nights*) is given as "three nights long." He also analyzes his own tendency to use "images which in order to augment an isolated thing multiply it by giving it plurality" ("La imagen que para engrandecer una cosa aislada la multiplica en numerosidad"). He then cites an illustrative line from his own poetry: "All the showy multitude of a sunset" ("Toda la charra multitud de un ocaso").[9]

Borges' literary infatuation with his native city and with his country—his *criollismo*—was especially evident at this point in his career. His prose, as well as his poetry of the period, reveal this fervent desire to capture the essence of Buenos Aires and the nation. In this sense several essays in *Inquisiciones* are companion pieces to his poetry. Even in an essay ostensibly dealing with European poetic trends, "La traducción de un incidente" ("Translation of an Incident"), he inserts a plea for a more genuine *criollista* orientation in Argentine poetry: "I believe that our verse should have a flavor of the *patria*, like a guitar that tastes of solitude, of the countryside and of sunset behind a field of clover" ("Creo que deberían nuestros versos tener sabor de patria, como guitarra que sabe a soledades y a campo y a poniente detrás de un trebolar").[10] One item in the collection, "Buenos Aires," is so imbued with Borges' poeticized view of the city that it can hardly be considered an essay; rather, it is a prose poem. As in his verse,

Borges describes how at sunset the city reveals itself, how "it is by dint of eventide that the city enters into us" ("Es a fuerza de tardes que la ciudad va entrando en nosotros").[11] In this same piece he writes of the close relationship between the Pampa and Buenos Aires—a theme which he reinforces in his well-known poem from *Fervor*, "La guitarra." In yet another *Inquisiciones* essay, "Queja de todo criollo" ("Native's Lament"), he continues this search for that which is essentially Argentine. He is cool toward writers like Lugones or Ricardo Güiraldes, who overemphasize the merely picturesque and whose work has an overt patriotic flavor. He believes that few writers have captured the distinctive traits of the Argentine character: an undercurrent of sadness and disillusionment along with a tendency to retreat from reality. To what extent these are part of the Argentine essence and to what extent they are projections of Borges' own personality would be difficult to determine.

Despite the occasional attacks on specific authors and movements, the bulk of the literary studies in *Inquisiciones* are not polemical in tone. Borges prefers the role of an observer rather than that of a preceptor. "I do not wish to set norms, but rather to set down observations" ("No quiero dictar normas, sino inscribir observaciones")[12] he writes in his essay on the poet Silva Valdés. In keeping with this position, his essays on Cansinos Assens, the Spanish *ultraísta*, on a group of nativist-gauchesque poets (Ipuche, Ascasubi), and on Ramón Gómez de la Serna, are descriptive rather than critical in character. Borges' ever-present interest in non-Hispanic literatures is seen in several pieces dedicated to Sir Thomas Browne, James Joyce, and Edward Fitzgerald. Like his essays on the preceding group of writers, these too are essentially sympathetic commentaries.

There are two remaining essays in *Inquisiciones* which merit special attention: "La nadería de la personalidad" ("The Nothingness of Personality") and "La encrucijada de Berkeley" ("Berkeley's Turning Point"). Both are philosophical rather than literary, both are sketchy formulations of ideas which were to dominate much of Borges' later work, and both were inspired by conversations with one of his most influential early mentors: the eccentric, little-known writer Macedonio Fernández.[13] In the first of these pieces Borges tries to show how the *yo*, the ego, as a discreet, identifiable entity has no reality. Ideas from Buddhism, Agrippa, and Schopenhauer are brought to bear on the central theme. In some mystical sense Borges (under the spell, no doubt, of Macedonio Fernández) agrees with Agrippa that the individual who attempts to express himself "wants to express life in its entirety" ("quiere expresar la vida entera").[14] There is a quality of "all-ness" in the ego: perhaps what Borges is saying may be reduced to the familiar notion of the ego as a microcosm of the universe. Toward the end of the essay, he seems to be especially attracted to Schopenhauer's idea of the ego as simply an "immovable point" which may serve as a vantage point from which to determine the flight of time. Viewed as a whole, the ideas in the essay do not fall into a clear or philosophically rigorous pattern, yet they do show a number of Borgesian themes in embryonic form. The microcosm idea—the notion of an entire life, or an entire universe being compressed into one point in space appears frequently in his fiction (in "El Aleph" and "La esfera de Pascal" ["Pascal's Sphere"], among others). The nothingness of the individual ego, along with the corresponding idea that the one is the all, were later to be expanded by Borges into themes of ambivalent personality, duplicated personality, and the like.

A good part of the "Encrucijada de Berkeley" consists of a rather routine sketch of the philosopher's essential ideas. Yet Borges, like many writers since Berkeley's time, wonders how the existence of mind itself may be posited if, in the Berkeleyan sense, it is the very means by which the entire universe exists. Borges appears to be dissatisfied with his understanding of the subtleties of this philosophic system. Thus, while the ideas of Berkeleyan idealism obviously fascinate him, he quite honestly writes that they are "more readily stated than understood" ("más aptas para ser dichas que para ser comprendidas").[15] This confession is significant: Borges makes no pretense of being a philosopher, yet he is very much attracted by the outward form of philosophic notions. Moreover, the fact that he may not thoroughly understand a particular concept does not inhibit his manipulating the concept in his literature. Witness the frequent touches of Berkeleyan idealism in his early poetry at a time when he clearly admits that he possessed more of a verbal familiarity with this philosophy than a genuine comprehension of it. Perhaps Borges has done what many of us do: perhaps he seized upon ideas only dimly seen, but by constantly using them, by accepting them *as if* he understood them profoundly, they became in a very real sense thoroughly learned.

II   El tamaño de mi esperanza

Borges' next collection of essays, *El tamaño de mi esperanza* (1926) contains some twenty-four pieces which deal in the main with themes of *criollismo* and, to a lesser extent, with analysis of poetic language. At no other point in his career was Borges so overtly concerned with defining the essence of the nation and even of the continent. The first essay, bearing the same title as that of the collection itself, begins with a ringing invocation: "I wish to speak to the *criollos:* to those men who feel themselves living and dying in this land, not to those who believe that the sun and moon are in Europe" ("A los criollos les quiero hablar: a los hombres que en esta tierra se sienten vivir y morir, no a los que creen que el sol y la luna están en Europa").[16] The polemical tone of this statement is carried through much of the essay; for example, he reproaches Sarmiento for being "North Americanized" of misunderstanding, and hating *lo criollo.* He again states that Argentina still has not produced any writer who has really fathomed the national essence in all its depth. Yet Borges warns against a restrictive jingoistic *criollismo* which would simply inflate national pride, isolate Argentinians, and cater to materialistic tendencies: "I desire neither progressivism nor *criollismo* in the current meaning of these words. . . . *Criollismo,* yes, but a *criollismo* which would be on speaking terms with the world, with the ego, with God and with death" ("No quiero ni progresismo ni criollismo en la acepción corriente de esas palabras. . . . Criollismo, pues, pero un criollismo que sea conversador del mundo y del yo, de Dios y de la muerte").[17] The bulk of the essays which follow are centered about this quest for an authentic but broad Argentinism: "El Fausto criollo" is a study of Del Campo's celebrated poem about the gaucho who goes to the famous opera; "La pampa y el suburbio son dioses" explains itself in its title, for in it Borges toys with the idea of man having "totems" even in the modern world; "Carriego y el sentido de arrabal" ("Carriego and the Meaning of Neighborhood") praises, perhaps overenthusiastically, Evaristo Carriego, a rather sentimental poet of Buenos Aires' neighborhoods; "Las coplas acriolladas" ("Nativized Verses") is a brief study of certain aspects of the region's folk poetry; and "Invectiva contra el arrabalero" ("Invective Against the *arrabalero*") is a critique of writers who try to create a feeling of authenticity in their work through the use of overly picturesque slang. As a group these pieces are not especially penetrating: they represent a period in Borges' career during which he felt a conscious need to explore and expound the *criollista* theme. As we shall see, his early reservations regarding overt *criollismo* gradually grew into an attitude based upon the conviction that one's expression of national or group identity need not, and should not, be deliberately set forth. As he observed in a later essay, the most obviously Arabic animal, the camel, does not appear even once in the Koran.[18]

The essays on poetics, language, and general literature in *El tamaño de mi esperanza* are by contrast with the *criollista* pieces, more revealing of the Borges which the world admires today. In his "Profesión de fe literaria" he continues his attack on rhyme, but more important, he voices an idea which is central to his view of literary art. Variety, he notes, is a specious quality, and only a few words or a few pages really matter to any writer. Borges presents, in effect, a good defense against the criticism that he frequently reworks themes, ideas, and even specific pages of earlier writings. If his ideas on variety are extended slightly, his views on literary originality may be better appreciated. Writers have a limited number of valid themes available to them, and literature may be conceived of as a finite body of material which the world's authors have reshuffled and rearranged; hence, originality itself becomes a questionable myth and to consider it the defining quality of good writing is untenable. Moreover, Borges was surprisingly sensitive to the fact that many writers (perhaps himself) occasionally repeat themselves or rework older material. In his very favorable review of Shaw's *St. Joan*, for example, he remarks "I haven't come upon the slightest bit of self-plagiarism, a thing at which my poverty is amazed" ("No he tropezado con el menor auto-plagio, cosa que mi pobreza se maravilla").[19] The reference to his own "poverty" may be significant: it indicated that Borges, even in 1926, felt that the range of his own literary talents was perhaps quite limited.

There are some grounds for Borges' sensitivity regarding self-plagiarism. A number of the essays in *El tamaño de mi esperanza* are remarkably similar to the pieces published in *Inquisiciones*:

certainly the themes parallel the earlier collection. In his discussion of rhyme—as in his scathing critique of a collection of Lugones' verse—he repeatedly makes the same points. And in the essay "Palabrería para versos" ("Wordiness for Verses") he actually interpolates in almost *verbatim* form several paragraphs from the "Examen de metáforas" which had already appeared in *Inquisiciones*.[20] These occasional duplications notwithstanding it would be an exaggeration to say that Borges did not add anything new to his analysis of poetic language in these essays. In two pieces, "Ejercicio de análisis" ("Exercise in Analysis") and "Examen de un soneto de Góngora," he demonstrates the problems and limitations of attempting to discover the essence of poetry by means of close textual analysis. In a third essay, "El idioma infinito" ("The Infinite Language"), he argues for enriching poetic language by all available means: the inclusion of new adjectives, verbs, and adverbs created from substantives; the freer use of prefixes and suffixes; the shift of verbs from their transitive to intransitive sense; and the use of terms in their etymological meaning.

The "Palabrería para versos," despite the repetition of some material written earlier, is the most significant essay of the collection since it deals with the difficult and fundamental question of the relationship of words to things. Borges makes one point in this essay which must be underscored. He notes that the single word is a kind of shorthand, an arbitrary summing-up, of complex impressions: by way of example he cites such ordinary nouns as "orange," "dagger," or "afternoon" and shows how each could be described by a lengthy circumlocution rather than by the conventional one-word term. It is a philosophical and linguistic commonplace to state that language may be described as an arbitrary set of symbols which do not have a one-for-one relationship to bits of clearly defined absolute reality—which is essentially what Borges is saying. But taken in the context of his literary development these ideas are very important. They foreshadow his interest in the philosophy of nominalism and they help explain some of the intricacies encountered by those readers of his fiction who journey with him to the strange world of Tlön.

Like his other early essay collections, *El tamaño de mi esperanza* is valuable to the student of Borges' literary trajectory in that it indicates what books he was reading and what ideas were coming to dominate his thought. In addition to the interest in the symbolic aspect of language, the genesis of another one of his philosophical concerns can be seen in the essay "Historia de los ángeles." Borges has had a consistent interest in Judaic culture; perhaps because of personal contacts with the large Buenos Aires Jewish community, perhaps because of some sentimental attachment stemming from the fact that he has some distant Jewish antecedents, or simply because he appreciates the rich intellectual contributions of this people. At any rate, both his poetry and prose give evidence of a surprisingly broad knowledge of Jewish folkways, traditions, and literature. The "Historia de los ángeles" is actually an extended book review of two volumes, Stehelin's *Rabbinical Literature* and Bischoff's *Elements of the Kabala*. The latter is the more important of the two since it shows Borges' early fascination with Jewish mysticism, numerology, and the like. Typically Kabalistic notions—the secret revelations of numerical relations, the world as a hidden cipher, and the mystic power of a code word—have played an especially important part in Borges' fiction, as readers of "El Aleph" or "La muerte y la brújula" soon discover; however, at this point in his literary development these ideas, like those on the nature of language, are in fragmentary form. They should be thought of as mere bits of "mental idlenesses" ("haraganerías del pensamiento"),[21] a phrase which Borges, in his characteristically offhand manner, uses to describe this entire collection.

III El idioma de los argentinos *and* Evaristo Carriego

Borges introduces his next book of essays, *El idioma de los argentinos* (1928), with a quotation from F. H. Bradley's *Appearance and Reality* and with a prologue in which he states that three themes dominate the work: "a fear, language . . . a mystery and a hope, eternity . . . this savor, Buenos Aires" ("Un recelo, el lenguaje . . . un misterio y una esperanza, la eternidad . . . esta gustación, Buenos Aires").[22] Borges' ordering of these three elements is not haphazard: it clearly shows the relative importance of each. Why Borges chose the word *recelo* (fear) to describe his attitude toward language is difficult to determine unless, perhaps, he wishes to emphasize its shade of meaning as "distrust." Poets especially, know that language is in a sense to be feared or distrusted, for it seems to jealously guard a realm of absolute reality just beyond the reach of the writer. Words, the basic unit of language, occupy Borges in the first essay of the collection, "Indagación de la palabra" ("A Study of the Word"). He finds that the "basic unit" may be more elusive than we expect, for the individual, disconnected word (*palabra suelta*) is purely arbitrary, and he shows that the identical thought can be handled by several different combinations of words. The particular material which he uses to illustrate the point is, incidentally, the first sentence of the *Don Quijote*. Borges, in effect, made the same point earlier in his "Palabrería para versos." In the present essay, however, the idea is further developed along lines suggested by his reading of Croce and of the psychologist, Spiller. The very last essay of the *Idioma de los argentinos*, and the one which gives the collection its title, deals with a closely related theme. Borges takes as his point of departure the idea that the urban slang of Buenos Aires (*lunfardo*) is of very limited value to writers and speakers of *porteño* Spanish simply because it only provides locally used synonyms for more generally accepted terms. The highly touted "lexical richness" of a language is a false value, for the mere variety of synonyms does not make a language express any wider range of reality than it would with fewer duplicating terms. Apparently Borges had by this time exhausted his ideas on the subject, for in the latter part of the piece he repeats (again virtually verbatim) that portion of the "Palabrería para versos" (from *El tamaño de mi esperanza*) which he had previously interpolated from the earlier essay "Examen de metáforas"! [23]

Borges' views on the nature and function of metaphor—another one of his major preoccupations throughout the 1920's—are considerably modified in one of the more extensive essays of *El Idioma de los argentinos*, "Otra vez la metáfora" ("The Metaphor Again"). He states at the outset that he does not believe that "metaphor making" is the fundamental task of the poet. Yet he notes parenthetically that he himself has been guilty of overestimating its importance—a reference, no doubt, to his *Ultraísta* theories. He goes on to show how very good poetry may be written with little or no recourse to metaphor and that metaphors may well be considered a luxury or mere adornment. In his attempt to evaluate the status of metaphor, Borges touches—although lightly —upon some important peripheral ideas. He states, for example, that "things are not intrinsically poetic; to raise them to poetry, we must link them to our existence, to accustom ourselves to think about them with devotion" ("Las cosas . . . no son intrínseca-mente poéticas; para ascenderlas a poesía, es preciso que los vin-culemos a nuestro vivir, que nos acostumbremos a pensarlas con devoción").[24] He goes on to suggest that there are two stages in the poetic process: the first of "poeticization," and the second of "exploitation." The metaphor is really not "poetic"; it is, Borges claims, "rather *postpoetic*, literary, and requires a very definitely preformed poetic state" (". . . la metáfora no es poética; es más bien *pospoética*, literaria, y requiere un estado de poesía ya for-madísimo").[25] As is frequently the case, Borges presents the start-ing point for what could be a very interesting discussion, but leaves the reader with little more than the suggestion of what might follow.

One of Borges' great strengths as a writer, and at the same time one of his greatest weaknesses, is the very quotable character of many of his lines. He is quite capable of writing a provocative, almost aphoristic, statement which seems to invite further discus-sion only to abandon the subject in the next line or to take another tack. Examples abound in the essays of this colllection. In "El cul-teranismo," a piece in praise of the highly Latinized poetry of Góngora, he parenthetically presents an extremely thought-provoking definition of poetry: "A conspiracy of men of good will to honor existence" ("Una conspiración hecha por hombres de buena voluntad para honrar el ser").[26] But the definition stands as it is, with Borges developing the theme no further. Another ex-ample is seen in "La felicidad escrita" ("Written Happiness") when he presents, but does not amplify, the statement that "the constant objective of literature is the presentation of destinies" ("la finalidad permanente de la literatura es la presentación de destinos").[27] Yet for those who have read Borges extensively these isolated maxims, definitions, or aphorisms have a much fuller meaning as well as inner consistency. But the fullness of meaning depends on our having seen how Borges uses a term such as "honor" in other contexts, or on having been initiated into the Borgesian sensitivity to the word "destiny" elsewhere. In short, the more familiar a reader is with Borges' total literary produc-tion, the less esoteric his work seems.

If an occasional isolated remark on the nature of literature strikes some readers as obscure, what Borges says of his specific

literary tastes in *El idioma de los argentinos* is certainly clear
enough. In one piece, "La fruición literaria," he even sketches out
his literary autobiography by enumerating his "greatest literary
pleasures." He lists the "dime novels" of Eduardo Gutiérrez,
Greek mythology, the *Estudiante de Salamanca,* the "very reason-
able and not at all fantastic fantasies of Jules Verne" ("Las tan
razonables y tan nada fantásticas fantasías de Julio Verne"), the
"grandiose" serial novels of Stevenson, and the "world's first in-
stallment novel" ("La primera novela por entregas del mundo"),
The Thousand and One Nights.[28] A second and more sophisticated
stage in the growth of his literary tastes came about with his "discovery of words." At this point, Borges tells us, he began reading
his "most frequently visited writers," Quevedo, Carlyle, Schopenhauer, Unamuno, and Dickens. This list is understandably incomplete since it is restricted primarily to those writers whom Borges
credits with having given him "pleasure." If he were to list also
those writers whose work interested him for other reasons, the list
would be long indeed. A casual remark near the end of this essay
is perhaps as revealing of Borges as the specific works he mentions. He very candidly says of these favorite books: "And today
. . . I re-read them with fond recollection, and new readings do
not arouse my enthusiasm" ("Y en el día de hoy . . . releo con
muy recordativo placer y que las lecturas nuevas no me entusi-
asman").[29] Recall that he was twenty-nine years of age at the time.
Yet Borges has read a staggering number of authors in addition to
the favorites noted in this essay; his book reviews and abundant
literary references attest this fact. There is, nonetheless, a fundamental conservatism in his makeup. His tendency to return to well-
remembered writers and well-worn themes, his reservations regarding originality and novelty, and his fascination with the
notion of repetition are all facets of this same essential characteristic.

   An unimportant-looking piece, buried amidst the impressive
and sophisticated literary criticism of the other essays in the
Idioma de los argentinos, bears out this view of Borges extremely
well. In the first place, it shows in a dramatic, almost poetic manner the author's obsessive desire to negate the flow of time. Secondly, it demonstrates Borges' tendency to reinsert a favorite page
into later writings which deal with similar themes. It is almost as
if Borges were trying to show his personal adherence to the idea

that there is nothing new under the sun. Titled "Sentirse en muerte" ("A Sense of Death") in this collection, this piece reappears in the title essay of the *Historia de la eternidad* (1936), and again in his essay of 1947, *Nueva refutación del tiempo.* With characteristic candor, Borges tells us in these later works that the piece dates from 1928. At the start of "Sentirse en muerte" Borges explains that there may be some readers who will understand his arguments on time and eternity more easily through his recounting a personal experience rather than by means of a technical philosophical presentation. What he retells in the essay will be familiar to many. He recalls one evening strolling through a neighborhood of Buenos Aires which he seldom frequented. Struck by the humble yet charming sight of typically old-fashioned *porteño* houses, surrounded by gardens and fig trees, Borges pauses to drink in the stillness of moonlight, the arched doorways and garden walls:

I remained staring at this simplicity. I thought, surely out loud: this is the same as thirty years ago. . . . The facile thought *I am somewhere in the Nineteenth Century* ceased to be a few approximate words and was deepened into reality. I felt dead, I felt that I was an abstract spectator of the world. . . . I did not think that I had returned upstream on the so-called waters of Time; rather I suspected that I was the possessor of an illusive or absent sense of the inconceivable word *eternity.* Only later did I succeed in defining that imagination.

(Me quedé mirando esa sencillez. Pensé, con seguridad en voz alta: Esto es lo mismo de hace treinta años. . . . El fácil pensamiento *Estoy en mil ochocientos y tantos* dejó de ser unas cuantas aproximativas palabras y se profundizó a realidad. Me sentí muerto, me sentí percibidor abstracto del mundo. . . . No creí no haber remontado las presuntivas aguas del Tiempo; más bien me sospeché poseedor del sentido reticiente o ausente de la inconcebible palabra *eternidad.*)[30]

What Borges wrote in 1928 requires no further comment and must be accepted—or rejected—at its face value. Borges' further attempts to intellectualize this moment of poetic vision, to justify it philosophically, or, as he put it, to "define that imagination" will be noted later. The importance of "Sentirse en muerte" lies in the fact that it is the earliest expression in prose of a key Borgesian theme and one that had figured prominently in his poetry of the 1920's. It points up his growing tendency to intellectualize in prose rather than simply express essentially poetic insights in verse.

Much of what Borges wrote in his next group of essays, collected under the title *Evaristo Carriego*, is a continuation of the "Sentirse en muerte" theme. The raw materials of the 1930 collection are the life and times of Carriego, a turn-of-the-century writer, greatly loved and appreciated by the Borges family, but who was something less than a major poet. The specific details of Carriego's life and the descriptions of the Palermo neighborhood in these essays are not as interesting to the general reader as is the way in which Borges handles what by now had become an obsession—his concern with time. Carriego's life, for example, is described as a "single day"; for a chronological series of events, Borges claims, cannot describe the unchanging, highly repetitive nature of his existence. In the case of a person such as Carriego we learn more by "looking for his eternity, his repetitions" ("es mejor buscar su eternidad, sus repeticiones").[31] *Evaristo Carriego* is one of the last works of Borges which centers on the nostalgic evocation of things past. As in much of the poetry of the 1920's Borges tries, almost in desperation, to freeze time, to hold fast to the memories of the Palermo of his childhood. A casual remark, in the second essay of the collection provides a touching finale to this phase of his work: "I possess memories of Carriego: memories of memories of other memories . . ." ("Poseo recuerdos de Carriego: recuerdos de recuerdos de otros recuerdos . . .").[32]

IV Discusión

Borges would probably prefer to be studied as he himself studied Carriego, not chronologically, but concentrating on the "identities," the repetitions in his life and works. Yet there is a historical dimension to his career and perhaps even genuine literary periods in his development. The changes in his poetry and the rather sudden decrease in his production of verse suggest that the early 1930's mark, in a real sense, a turning point, if not a crisis in his life as a writer. The essays in *Discusión* (1932) confirm this view. Yet it would be incorrect to claim that a "new" Borges emerges during this period, for his essential preoccupations and his basic literary outlook remain what they were in the 1920's.

What changes is Borges' emphasis and to a degree his manner of expression. The intellectualization—hinted at in such early essays as "La encrucijada de Berkeley"—now comes out in full flower; his tendency to escape the here and the now through memory and poetic evocation gives way to a greater interest in the arcane, the esoteric, and the exotic. Finally, as his fiction begins to develop, fantasy, irony, and humor come to be major weapons in his literary arsenal.

The lead essay in *Discusión*, "Nuestras imposibilidades," is one of the least typical pieces Borges has ever produced. In a more recent edition of the collection (1955) it has been omitted, with a note stating that "it would now seem very weak" ("El artículo . . . ahora parecería muy débil"). Borges' dismay in the face of the events which followed the fall of the Irigoyen government no doubt prompted him to write this unusual essay. In it he bitterly attacks the "everyday Argentine" by pointing out "certain not-so-glorious aspects of our character" ("ciertos caracteres de nuestro ser que no son tan gloriosos").[33] He singles out the typical *porteño*'s hypocrisy, by observing how he denigrates the United States while he boasts that Buenos Aires rivals Chicago in the violence of its criminals. He chastizes his compatriots for their lack of imagination and for their tendency to enjoy seeing people humiliated. Finally, in an unusual display of political invective, he berates "a conservative government which is forcing the republic into socialism only to annoy and demoralize a middle party" ("un gobierno conservador, que está forzando a toda la república a ingresar en el socialismo, sólo por fastidiar y entristecer a un partido medio").[34] The specific ills which he points out and the exact political position he expresses are less significant than is the fact that he was sufficiently aroused to use his pen for direct social and political criticism. The case is almost unique; perhaps it indicates that Borges was, to use the well-worn expression, not himself.

Considering Borges' disenchantment with the Argentina and the Buenos Aires of the period, it is not surprising that of the sixteen essays in the original collection only two would touch upon local themes. The contrast with his earlier collections could not be sharper. The dominating themes of *Discusión* are mystic cosmology, problems involving space and time, and the application—or misapplication—of the causality concept to literature. Though Borges had always sprinkled his essays with references to

his favorite authors, his amazingly broad familiarity with books
and writers—including many that his readers could hardly be expected to know—becomes especially evident in this collection. A
fascinating procession marches through the book's pages: ancient
heresiarchs such as Basilides or Valentius, the churchman Ireneus,
philosophers like Spencer, Bergson and Russell, followed by a
host of famous literary figures—Novalis, Rimbaud, William
Morris, Whitman, and Melville.

Borges had hinted at his interest in the cosmology and metaphysics of the Gnostics in his earlier writings.[35] But in his essay
"Una vindicación del falso Basilides" his exploration of the subject
becomes a central concern: with typical frankness he begins the
piece by telling his readers exactly how he first became interested
in this unusual philosophy. As a youth of seventeen, he happened
upon Quevedo's work on the Gnostic heresies; shortly afterward,
while in Europe, he read the German version of George Mead's
rich anthology of Gnostic thought, *Fragments of a Faith Forgotten*, as well as various encyclopedia articles. This philosophical
tradition is too vast, too complex, and too varied to be outlined
here: those who would like to follow its threads through Borges'
prose might profit by reading Mead's volume, apparently his main
source of information. Among the intricacies of Gnosticism several
ideas seem to hold a special fascination for Borges: the notion of a
creator "behind" the creator, with the implication that the God of
the main Judeo-Christian tradition is merely an "intermediary," a
much lesser being—perhaps even the adversary of the true Master; the concept of an almost infinite number of angels, gods, demi-
gods, and intermediaries inhabiting the cosmos; the suggestion of
a creator behind a creator, behind a creator, and so on; the notion
of a multiplicity of possible worlds; and finally, the view of the
world's coming into existence quite haphazardly, as the mere
whim of a "minor" creator.

Borges was, no doubt, charmed by the absurdity of the vast and
weighty polemics to which the Gnostic heresies have given rise
through the centuries. What rich possibilities are suggested if we
assume, for the purpose of our literary and intellectual pleasure,
that the Gnostics were right, that they indeed possessed the inner
vision of the cosmos which they claimed! As Borges notes, in that
case Novalis' idea that "life is a sickness of the spirit" or Rimbaud's notion that "True life is absent; [and that] we are not in

the world" might then have canonical justification.[36] The essay on Basilides is one of the few pieces in which Borges deals with Gnosticism directly; however, this tradition helps shape much of his fiction, as can readily be seen in such stories as "Las ruinas circulares" or "Tres versiones de Judas."

"Una vindicación de la Cábala," written in 1931 and included in *Discusión,* may be thought of as a companion piece to the essay on Basilides, since the roots of both the Kabala and the gnosis are intimately entwined in the mystery cults of the ancient Near East. Despite its title, the piece deals more with a cabalistic approach to Christian Scripture than it does with the content of this famous compendium of Hebraic numerology, mysticism, and ancient lore. Borges focuses his attention upon the problem of the exact meaning of the Trinity and especially upon the significance of the term "Holy Ghost." He conjectures that the phrase may be merely a syntactical form and that "what is certain is that the third blind person of the tangled trinity is the recognized author of the Scriptures" ("lo cierto es que la tercera ciega persona de la enredada trinidad es el reconocido autor de las Escrituras").[37] If this is so, Borges continues, the Scriptures are indeed "dictated"; they are complete, and contain no gratuitous or chance elements. At the essay's conclusion Borges further hypothesizes that if we grant this completeness and the necessity of every scriptural detail, then we might find, by applying the cabalistic method of treating divine writing as a code, that every detail, every word, every number in the Scriptures has a secret, unrevealed meaning. Curiously, the essay ends abruptly at this point. But Borges' interest in Judaic literature—particularly in its more mystical manifestations —was to reappear many times again in his work. In another essay of *Discusión,* "El otro Whitman" ("The Other Whitman") he tries to characterize the breadth, the all-encompassing quality of the North American's poetry by citing a passage from the Hebrew *Zohar* in which the vastness and omnipresence of God is described. And in his fiction such famous pieces as "El milagro secreto" ("The Secret Miracle") and "La muerte y la brújula," ("Death and the Compass") attest his great fascination for Judaic culture.

Those who criticize Borges for his intellectuality, for his cold and formalistic literature, have probably formed their opinion on a basis of having read—among other similar Borgesian compositions—the concluding essay in *Discusión*, "La perpetua carrera de Aquiles y la tortuga" ("The Perpetual Race of Achilles and the Tortoise"). The subject of the piece is Zeno's Second Paradox; or more accurately, the Aristotelian version of the famous problem. The swift Achilles (who presumably runs at a rate ten times that of his rival) gives the tortoise a ten-meter head start while he waits at the starting point. He then runs the ten meters while the tortoise runs one; Achilles then runs a meter while the tortoise covers a tenth of a meter; he then covers a tenth of a meter, while his rival runs a mere hundredth of a meter; and so on. Obviously, though the distance between the two gets infinitely small, Achilles can never overtake the tortoise. As in all good mathematical paradoxes, we sense the absurdity of what seems mathematically irrefutable. Most people will dismiss this sort of problem after a few moment's reflection. But not Borges. He finds in it a glimpse of the inconceivable notion of infinity, a concept which he once described as the one which "corrupts and upsets all others" ("un concepto . . . corruptor y . . . desatinador de los otros").[38] In fact Borges was so taken with this paradox—and other forms of the same problem—that he devotes several pages to analyzing the attempts of such thinkers as Mill, Bergson, Russell, and James to solve it. His critique of the various solutions seems sophisticated and well-taken, but could only be properly evaluated by a logician. At the conclusion he remains unsatisfied with the explanations supplied by these illustrious minds: "Zeno is unanswerable," he tells us, "unless we confess the ideality of space and time. Let us accept idealism. Let us accept the concrete growth of that which is perceived and we will avoid the pullulation of the paradox's abysses" ("Zenón es incontestable, salvo que confesemos la idealidad del espacio y del tiempo. Aceptemos el idealismo, aceptemos el crecimiento concreto de lo percibido, y eludiremos la pululación de abismos de la paradoja").[39] Yet Borges was still not completely satisfied with his own solution: several years later he returned to the problem in another essay, and reflections of it haunt much of his prose. In his obsessive return to the ideas of infinitely smaller units, of infinitely branching paths, and of the endlessly repeated images of the double mirror Borges shows a curious blend of childish delight, esthetic awe, and mathematical passion. To the extent that his readers share these reactions, they will appreciate this aspect of his work.

Not all the essays of *Discusión* are as abstract as the one just discussed, yet even those which treat more concrete subjects are infused with an intellectual intensity—with an almost mathematical rigor—that is not nearly as evident in Borges' earlier essays, for example, when he describes our present knowledge of Homer, in "Las versiones homéricas" ("Homeric Translations"), he writes that "The present state of his works seems to be like a complicated equation which gives precise relations between unknown quantities" ("El estado presente de sus obras es parecido al de una complicada ecuación que registra relaciones precisas entre cantidades incógnitas").[40]

Other essays on literature in *Discusión* reveal an interest in plot and structure which suggest a mathematician's appreciation of formal elegance. "El arte narrativo y la magia" ("Narrative Art and Magic") illustrates this concern as well as Borges' views on the problems of narration. The essay is especially important since it was composed just before he began writing his first short stories. He begins the essay by discussing Poe, William Morris, and Milville. He states that what he likes in these authors is the "secret plot," the arcane element which one may discover in their work. In contrast to the work of these few writers much of the typical fiction of the same period—the mid-nineteenth century—falls into the category of "the draggy novel of characters" ("la morosa novela de caracteres").[41] By contrast, the ideal novel should be "a precise game of staying on the alert, of echoes, and of affinities" ("un juego preciso de vigilancias, ecos y afinidades").[42] Borges points out an example of this kind of fiction in a story of Chesterton and then sums up the alternatives with which any writer of narrative fiction is faced: "I have contrasted two causal processes: the natural one, which is the incessant result of uncontrollable and infinite operations; (and) the lucid and limited magical one, wherein the details are prophetic. In the novel, I feel that the only possible honesty lies in the second alternative. Leave the first to psychological fakery" ("He distinguido dos procesos causales: el natural, que es el resultado incesante de incontrolables e infinitas operaciones; el mágico, donde profetizan los pormenores, lúcido y limitado. En la novela pienso que la única posible honradez está con el segundo. Quede el primero para la simulación psicológica").[43]

The full impact of this sweeping division of novelists into sheep and goats, which this statement implies, may be difficult to appreciate at first glance. Borges is in effect saying that the "psychological" novel, and all fiction which develops its structure from the interplay of personalities (personality viewed in toto) should be relegated to the category of "fakery." He holds, and with some justification, that the infinitude of events, causal factors, "influences" and the like which constitute a single human life are so complex that the writer who attempts to build a work of fiction on such material is pretentious and dishonest. Rather, he suggests that writers abandon attempts for psychological realism in fiction, limit their material, organize it, and emphasize the narrative element by structuring detail to fit a preconceived (perhaps even a secret, "held-back") pattern. In a word, novelists should aim at producing "a precise game of vigilances, echoes and 'affinities.'" Borges thus presents a manifesto of prose fiction, and a defense of his own, but as yet unwritten, work in the genre. The essay may also help explain why a substantial number of readers and critics —especially devotees of psychological literature—cannot accept him as a great prose writer.

V Historia de la eternidad *and* Nueva refutación del tiempo

The *Historia de la eternidad* (1936), contains only six compositions, one of which, "El acercamiento a Almotásim" ("The Approach to Almotasim") is usually treated as an example of Borges' fiction. Another, "Las kenningar," appeared in 1933 as a separately published essay, though it is only several pages in length. Its appeal must be considered quite limited, since it does little more than list a large number of *kenningar:* conventional poetic figures which appear in ancient Icelandic sagas. Borges makes some comments on the nature of metaphor in the piece, but confesses that one of his chief reasons for his interest in the subject is "the almost philatelic pleasure" he felt while gathering the material. Those of us who are not stamp collectors may not share his enthusiasm.

The title essay of *Historia de la eternidad* is Borges' longest effort in the genre. He devotes approximately forty pages to a compilation of many of his ideas on the flow of time, idealism, and the meaning of eternity. Despite its length, or perhaps because of it, the essay lacks the brilliance and concision of some of his other writings on the same subject. Borges makes rather generous use of material drawn from earlier essays: a substantial section of "Una vindicación de la Cábala" appears in it as does the complete "Sentirse en muerte." In the first part of the essay he discusses some of the traditional views of time, viewing it first as a current flowing in either direction, then as an eternal archetype, or as a Platonic ideal. About halfway through the essay Borges playfully remarks: "I was about to forget another archetype which exalts and includes all others: eternity, whose shattered copy is time" ("Me olvidaba de otro arquetipo que los comprende a todos y los exalta: la eternidad, cuya despedezada copia es el tiempo").[44] This image is difficult indeed to imagine and in the material following, Borges does little to further our understanding of it. At this point in the essay the author presents some fascinating, but not especially helpful, digressions. He shows how the terms "creation" and "conservation" are synonymous in a Berkeleyan Heaven, and how if the God of the Idealists were to shift his attention for one second away from Borges' hand, it would disappear. Toward the essay's conclusion, the author informs his readers that he wishes to present his own version of eternity which is "By now without God, and even without another possessor and without archetypes" ("Ya sin Dios, y aun sin otro poseedor y sin arquetipos").[45] To clarify the essential meaning of this eternity he then repeats the entire "Sentirse en muerte" from *El idioma de los argentinos*. Borges seems to be saying that neither he nor his reader are really convinced by this lengthy philosophical discussion of time and eternity: hence, almost in defeat, he utilizes the simple personal experience recounted in the earlier piece.

Of the remaining essays in the collection several are sufficiently important to be noted in a general study of his work. Of these, "La doctrina de los ciclos" is especially interesting since it touches upon a key Borgesian theme—the relation of time and infinity. He begins the piece by examining such mathematical and physical concepts as the laws of thermodynamics and the idea of entropy. Borges comes to the conclusion that if we have a universe with finite matter and infinite time, sooner or later things get back to a "repeated" state and that then the cycle begins to work itself out once again. He concludes this rather complex essay by noting that there is no "practical" concern in all this. Though this observation may be correct, the essay is noteworthy since it sheds light on such pieces as the poem "La noche cíclica" or the story "La biblioteca de Babel," both of which are based on the same central idea.

Only thirty-three pages in length, Borges' next essay, the "Nueva refutación del tiempo" (1947), constitutes one of his most representative works. In a very real sense Borges had been writing this essay during his entire life, and perhaps he is still writing it. His fondness for literary hoaxes and bookish trickery notwithstanding, Borges is a very honest writer, a fact which this essay makes quite clear. He explains, in the prologue to the "Neuva refutación," that it is a two-part essay, the first half of which had appeared in *Sur* in 1944. He admits that in the present day and age his ideas are an "anachronistic *reductio ad absurdum* of a preterite system" ("la anacrónica *reductio ad absurdum* de un sistema pretérito").[46] He also notes that the very title contains a logical fallacy, for how can time be "refuted" when the temporal term "New" is used as a modifier of the word "time"? Borges' essential candor is again seen in the first paragraph of the essay when he says that in the course of his life "I have glimpsed . . . a refutation of time, in which I myself do not believe, but which regularly visits me at night and in the weary twilight with the illusory force of an axiom" ("He divisado . . . una refutación del tiempo, de lo que yo mismo descreo, pero que suele visitarme en las noches y en el fatigado crepúsculo, con ilusoria fuerza de axioma").[47] He then notes some of the many places in his writings where this obsessive desire to refute time comes to the surface, though he discerningly points out that in "some way or another" it is to be found in all his books. Yet he openly states that he is not satisfied with his previous attempts to set forth the refutation. He characterizes his most ambitious attempt in this direction, the *Historia de la eternidad* as "less demonstrative and well-reasoned than it is divinatory and pathetic" ("menos demostrativo y razonado que adivinatorio y patético")[48]—a singularly honest evaluation with which many will be forced to agree.

The "Nueva refutación . . ." is written in a closely knit and rigorous style. It admits little condensation and should be read in its entirety. At the risk of doing the essay and Borges an injustice, a few salient points may, however, be extracted. The first of these is that once we accept the negation of the "continuities" of matter, spirit, and space, it follows that the continuity of time may be—or must be—negated. The route by which Borges leads his reader through Berkeley and Hume to this point is strewn with rocks and confused by such intersecting side roads as the one marked "Schopenhauer's dualism: Do not enter." To reinforce his negation of time's continuity, Borges resorts to a number of "common-sense" arguments, the bulk of which revolve about the idea that two events occuring at what we would call the same moment in time may only be "contemporary" in historical retrospect. When Borges' ancestor, Captain Isidoro Suárez was leading an attack in Peru early in August, 1824, De Quincey was publishing a book in London. The two men died in complete ignorance of each other. These and other examples lead Borges to ask "if time is a mental process, how can thousands of men—or even two different men—share it?" ("Si el tiempo es un proceso mental¿ cómo pueden compartirlo millares de hombres, o aun dos hombres distintos?").[49] At the close of the first part of the essay (the section written in 1944) Borges, as always desperately trying to convince himself and his reader of something in which he admittedly "does not believe," employs two tactics. He first absolves himself for not being able to communicate his analysis of time on the ground that language is by its very nature an inadequate instrument for the discussion of time, and secondly, he makes a last-ditch attempt at getting his point over by reprinting—once again—the "Sentirse en muerte" fragment of 1928.

The second section (text "B") of the "Nueva refutación" was written in 1947, some three years after the first part. Borges explains that in it he wishes to do exactly what he wished to do in the first part but that he deliberately did not fuse the two essays into one, since "the reading of two analagous texts might facilitate the comprehension of an indocile topic" ("la lectura de dos textos análogos puede facilitar la comprensión de una materia indócil").[50] Thus "B" follows the same general lines as the earlier text: Berkeleyan idealism is again explained, and its misinterpretations noted. Borges places considerable emphasis on extending Hume's idea—also implicit in Berkeley—that the self can be considered a bundle or collection of different perceptions which succeed each other with an inconceivable rapidity. In his attempt to deny the existence of time, or perhaps in his desire to redefine it as merely the consciousness of the present moment, Borges tries to manipulate Hume's denial of the metaphysical notion of "self" and to incorporate into his own thinking the same philosopher's concept of time as "a succession of indivisible moments." But as in text "A" of the essay, both author and reader seem to become hopelessly entangled in this fine-spun reasoning.

An important difference in the 1947 portion of the essay as compared with the earlier text is in the choice of exemplary material. In text "B" Borges uses the ancient Chinese tale of Chuang Tzu, the man who dreamt he was a butterfly and upon waking did not know if he indeed was a man who dreamt he was a butterfly or a butterfly who was now dreaming that he was a man. He also employs certain figurative passages from Buddhist literature, as well as miscellaneous quotations from Plutarch, Schopenhauer, and F. H. Bradley. All point to the reality of the present moment and to the logical necessity of denying the existence of past or future. Though all these arguments are far from convincing, the essay's last paragraph is one of the most quotable Borges has ever written. Its ironies can, perhaps, only be appreciated after one has fought along with Borges in this magnificent and futile struggle:

And yet, and yet . . . Denying temporal succession, denying the self, denying the astronomical universe, are apparent desperations and secret consolations. Our destiny (as contrasted with the hell of Swedenborg and the hell of Tibetan mythology) is not frightful by being unreal; it is frightful because it is irreversible and iron-clad. Time is the substance I am made of. Time is a river which sweeps me along, but I am the river; it is a tiger which destroys me, but I am the tiger; it is a fire which consumes me, but I am the fire. The world, unfortunately, is real; I, unfortunately, am Borges.

(And yet, and yet . . . Negar la sucesión temporal, negar el yo, negar el universo astronómico, son desesperaciones aparentes y consuelos secretos. Nuestro destino [a diferencia del infierno de Swedenborg y del infierno de la mitología tibetana] no es espantoso por irreal; es espantoso porque es irreversible y de hierro. El tiempo es la substancia de que estoy hecho. El tiempo es un río que me arrebata, pero yo soy el río; es un tigre que me destroza, pero yo soy el tigre; es un fuego que me consume, pero yo soy el fuego. El mundo, desgraciadamente, es real; yo, desgraciadamente, soy Borges.)[51]

VI   Otras inquisiciones

To discuss Borges' other essays after having tackled the formidable "Nuestra refutación" may seem anticlimactic. Yet his last major collection, *Otras inquisiciones* (1952), contains a number of pieces which are indispensable parts of a complete view of his works as essayist. The collection includes some thirty-nine pieces, covering the period 1937–52; hence, it is difficult to generalize about its contents. Almost all the essays take major literary figures or their works as their point of departure. In addition to pieces on old favorites (Chesterton, Quevedo, Whitman, Cervantes) several less-frequented authors make their appearance: Pascal, Coleridge, Kafka, Hawthorne, Leon Bloy, and Valery. A few of the essays in the collection are focused on philosophical questions rather than on literary matters, though for a writer of Borges' temperament the two areas are virtually inseparable.

Borges, who has never written a novel, has a good deal to say about the genre. Like a number of other contemporary writers— the Mexican, Octavio Paz, for example—he has a certain distrust of it, and perhaps considers the modern novel a degenerated product of more praiseworthy literary forms. The *Otras inquisiciones* contains several pieces which treat this theme, though he had already discussed it elsewhere: his essay of 1932, "El arte narativo y la magia," it will be recalled, is one of his earliest pronouncements on the subject. Several of his uncollected pieces also show his preferences quite clearly. In one such piece—a book review of Faulkner's *Absalom, Absalom!*—he pays the North American novelist high tribute by noting that he (like Joseph Conrad) has the rare talent of being on the one hand "profoundly human" and on the other, of being a "pure" artist in the sense that his "central concern is for verbal procedures" (". . . su central ansiedad son los procedimientos verbales"). Most important, Borges reveals a critical attitude toward the very successful novelist who is not much concerned with formal structure, but whose work is based simply on "the passions and doings of man" ("las pasiones y trabajos del hombre"). This kind of writer, he observes, is "more fortunate and knows the laudatory epithets 'profound,' 'human,' 'profoundly human' " ("más feliz y conoce los epítetos laudatorios 'profundo,' 'humano,' 'profundamente humano' ").[52] A newspaper review of Hugh Walpole's murder mystery *The Killer and the Slain* (another item which has not appeared in any of the collections) sheds more light on his attitude toward the novel. In this piece he again reveals his fondness for detective fiction and similarly highly structured narratives; but the most interesting part of

the review comes when Borges applies to novels Edgar Allan
Poe's idea that there is really no such thing as a "long poem": "this
argument is transferable to prose and it could be reasoned that
the novel is not a literary genre but rather a mere typographical
phantom" ("ese argumento es trasladable a la prosa y cabría
razonar que la novela no es un género literario sino un mero simu-
lacro tipográfico").[53]

When Borges questions the very existence of the genre he
shows, although in an exaggerated way, his low evaluation of a
great many highly regarded novels of the modern period. His
preferences in longer prose fiction are for allegory, romance, and,
of course, the detective tale. Thus in *Otras inquisiciones* he seems
to take almost perverse pleasure in writing glowingly on William
Beckford's *Vathek*, a rather obscure Gothic novel known chiefly to
students of eighteenth-century letters. On the other hand, he either ignores or treats casually many of the major novelists of the
past two centuries. Even when he discusses an important novelist,
he tends to praise lesser-known compositions or subtle details in
major works. In his essay on Hawthorne—given first as a lecture
in 1949 but included in *Otras inquisiciones*—he notes that the
American writer devises situations first and then lets his characters
in a sense "play out" the roles demanded by the situation. This
method, he states "may produce . . . admirable stories . . . but
not admirable novels" ("Ese método puede producir . . . admirables cuentos . . . pero no admirables novelas").[54] Hence, he
apparently prefers Hawthorne's short fiction; for example, a story
such as "Wakefield," rather than *The Scarlet Letter* or *The House
of Seven Gables*. Borges' penchant for praising an unusual detail
in a well-known work is especially evident in his comments on
Don Quijote. Rather than the broad human sweep of Cervantes'
masterpiece, what he decides to discuss is the fact that Don Quijote himself (in the ninth chapter) reads the *Don Quijote*. Thus in
"Magias parciales del Quijote" he playfully observes, "these inver-
sions suggest that if the characters of a work of fiction can be
readers or spectators, we readers or spectators may be fictitious"
("tales inversiones sugieren que si los caracteres de una ficción
pueden ser lectores o espectadores nosotros sus lectores o espectadores podemos ser ficticiosos").[55] In several other essays in *Otras
inquisiciones* Borges reveals his strong opinions on the novel: in
"De las alegorías a las novelas" ("From Allegories to Novels"), in

which he discusses the modern shift away from allegory by contrasting the ideas of Croce and Chesterton, in the various essays on Wells, Kafka, or Chesterton, and elsewhere. One of his clearest, most provocative denunciations of the modern novel, and indeed of most contemporary literature, appears in the "Nota sobre (hacia) Bernard Shaw" ("A note on [Toward] Bernard Shaw"). Significantly, Shaw whom he praises highly, is not a novelist. Borges tells us that Shaw, like the poet Valery, who is also lauded in *Otras inquisiones,* is one of the few moderns who has not surrendered to the "immoral" cult of sentimentality, desperation, anguish, and existentialism. The eloquent and lucid final paragraph of the "Nota sobre (hacia) Bernard Shaw" bears citing in its entirety:

> Man's character and its variations are the essential theme of the novel of our time; lyric poetry is the complacent magnification of amorous fortunes or misfortunes; the philosophies of Heidegger and Jaspers make each of us the interesting interlocutor in a secret and continuous dialogue with nothingness or the divinity; these disciplines, which in the formal sense can be admirable, foment that illusion of the ego which the Vedanta censures as a capital error. They usually make a game of desperation and anguish, but at bottom they flatter our vanity; they are, in this sense, immoral. The work of Shaw, however, leaves one with a flavor of liberation. The flavor of the Stoic doctrines and the flavor of the sagas.

> (El carácter del hombre y sus variaciones son el tema esencial de la novela de nuestro tiempo; la lírica es la complaciente magnificación de venturas o desventuras amorosas; las filosofías de Heidegger y de Jaspers hacen de cada uno de nosotros el interesante interlocutor de un diálogo secreto y continuo con la nada o con la divinidad; estas disciplinas, que formalmente pueden ser admirables, fomentan esa ilusión del yo que el Vedanta reprueba como error capital. Suelen jugar a la desesperación y a la angustia, pero en el fondo halagan la vanidad; son, en tal sentido, inmorales. La obra de Shaw, en cambio, deja un sabor de liberación. El sabor de las doctrinas del Pórtico y el sabor de las sagas.) [56]

Given this attitude, small wonder that readers of Borges should find no studies on such novelists as Dostoevsky, Tolstoy, Camus, or Sartre in his books, much less any serious lines about compatriots like Eduardo Mallea or Ernesto Sábato. Borges offers a final remark on the novel as a literary form in a later essay, "Vindicación de *Bouvard et Pécuchet*" (1954). Although his point of departure is Flaubert's unfinished, and relatively unknown novel, he seems more interested in Chesterton's idea that "the novel may well die with us." Borges adds that Chesterton could be correct and that if he were, Joyce's *Ulysses* might then be considered "the splendid death-agony" ("la esplendida agonía") of the genre.[57]

As Borges himself has remarked, all of his books deal—at least in some measure—with time. *Otras inquisiciones* is no exception. In addition to the "Nueva refutación del tiempo," which was reprinted in the collection, at least half a dozen other pieces take up various aspects of the subject. Yet compared with his major effort of 1947, these essays appear to be mere skirmishes with the enemy rather than full-scale battles. Two pieces, each based on the ideas of rather obscure amateur philosophers are typical. In "El tiempo y J. W. Dunne" ("Time and J. W. Dunne") he stresses Dunne's notion that after death each individual will be free to rearrange every instant of his life as he may wish. In "La creación de P. H. Gosse" he takes up the bizarre ideas of an eccentric thinker who held that at some point in the world's evolution the idea of God's creation of the universe was interjected and that as a result, the fossils we find may be real enough, but the beasts who caused them didn't exist! At the root of the ideas of both Gosse and Dunne is essentially the same inconceivable suggestion that the normal temporal succession of events may, in some manner, have been altered. Intrigued more than convinced, Borges characterizes Gosse's thought as having "a rather monstrous elegance" ("una elegancia un poco monstruosa").[58]

Somewhat similar notions on time are woven into a number of the more literary essays of *Otras inquisiciones*. In "La flor de Coleridge" he analyzes several techniques for creating fantastic effects through the manipulation of time: Coleridge's use of a flower which appears first in a dream and then later is present when the dreamer awakes; H. G. Wells's insertion of the "withered flower of the future" in his novel *The Time Machine;* and finally, Henry James's analysis of the possible effects on the present that might result from a trip to the past, as seen in his time-travel story, "The Sense of the Past." One of the most provocative pieces in the collection, "Kafka y sus precursores" approaches the question of chronological sequence in an unusual manner. Taken out of context, Borges' statement in the essay that "every writer *creates* his precursors" ("cada escritor *crea* a sus precursores") seems deliberately illogical. Yet what he says is both logical and historically valid, though some may consider it a truism. Borges begins the essay by showing how such dissimilar authors as Zeno, Browning, Leon Bloy, and Kierkegaard have all written certain pages in which a person familiar with Kafka would note a particular idiosyncrasy typical of this modern Czech master. "But if Kafka had never written a line," Borges explains, "we would not perceive this quality, it would not exist" ("Pero si Kafka no hubiera escrito . . . no la percibiríamos . . . no existiría"). Following a thought suggested by T. S. Eliot, Borges sums up his point: "[Every writer's] work modifies our conception of the past, as it will modify the future" ("Su labor modifica nuestra concepcíon del pasado, como ha de modificar el futuro").[59]

Closely akin to the time theme is Borges' long-standing exploration of the notion of infinitude, evident in this collection in several essays. Even in pieces in which his primary concern is for seemingly unrelated matters, ideas of infinite series, infinite division of time or space into increasingly smaller units, or the opposing—but equally disturbing—notion of a closed, finite universe, intrigue him. The fact that in the *Quijote* the hero himself reads the book suggests an infinite series of items contained within other items. This detail in Cervantes' famous work reminds Borges of Josiah Royce's reference to the English monarch who had so huge a map of his kingdom made that on the map itself the map-in-miniature again appeared, and on this map, a smaller map, and so on. Another expression of Borges' fascination with infinitude is seen in his interest in problems of a mathematical sort involving "convergences": the best example is again the paradox of Achilles and his race with the tortoise. The famous contest, it may be recalled, was first celebrated by Borges in his collection of 1932, *Discusión*. It reappears, and in perhaps more rigorous form, in an essay of 1939, "Avatares de la tortuga," included in *Otras inquisiciones*. Here Borges develops the idea that the "vertiginous" *regressus in infinitum* suggested by the paradox, "may be applicable to everything" ("es acaso aplicable a todos los temas")—to literature, the problem of knowledge, and so on. The only philosophical tradition which seems to supply a satisfactory explanation for such paradoxes is that of idealism, which admits "the hallucinatory nature of the world" (el carácter alucinatorio del mundo"). Our dream of the world, Borges goes on to explain, though it may be "firm, mysterious, visible, ubiquitous in space and durable in time" nonetheless shows "tenuous and eternal crevices of unreason which tell us it is false" ("Nosotros . . . hemos soñado el mundo. Lo hemos soñado resistente, misterioso, visible, ubicuo en el espacio y firme en el tiempo; pero hemos consentido en su arquitectura tenues y eternos intersticios de sinrazón para saber que es falso").[60] Unexplainable paradoxes and inconceivable notions such as that of infinity presumably constitute these "crevices of unreason."

If we apply the concept of infinitude to the world, if we say that all things are infinitely divisible, then the symbols which we use to describe the world—language—may also be thought of as infinitely divisible. This idea has come up earlier in Borges' essays; in *Otras inquisiciones* it appears, perhaps just below the surface, in "El idioma analítico de John Wilkins." In the seventeenth century, Wilkins wrote a treatise on "Philosophical Language" in which he proposed an organized synthetic language. His attempt had all the artificial and arbitrary qualities which any synthetic tongue has. Borges uses the work of this obscure writer as a point of departure to discuss a variety of curious, and often very humorous, attempts of a similar nature. The point of the essay seems to be that language—even naturally evolved language—is no more than an arbitrary system whose "units" may stand for a large segment of what we call reality, or for a minuscule segment. The use of generic linguistic symbols as opposed to specific ones is likewise conventional rather than logically necessary. The essay further suggests the idea, perhaps related to the philosophy of nominalism, that we only delude ourselves if we think of any language as describing all of reality's infinite bits and pieces.

Borges' continued interest in mysticism, in unusual cosmologies, and especially in Gnosticism is also very evident in *Otras inquisiciones*. Since theological questions often revolve upon comments upon comments, his reading of a particular author frequently sets off a chain reaction of ideas which ultimately leads to his own personal interpretation. "El Biathanatos" is a case in point, since it was inspired by De Quincey's comments on an essay written by

John Donne. The subject of the piece is suicide, which Donne treated as a special case of justifiable homicide. De Quincey suggests that Donne may well have wished to present, in a thinly veiled manner, the thesis that Christ's death was such a case. The enormity of this idea prompts Borges to place the entire question within a Gnostic frame of reference and to express his fascination with the thought of "a god who builds the universe in order to build his own scaffold" ("un dios que fabrica el universo para fabricar su patíbulo").[61] "El espejo de los enigmas" is somewhat like the foregoing in that it too is a comment on a comment. The text in question is the well-known verse from St. Paul in which our view of the world is described as being "as through a glass darkly." Leon Bloy, the French Catholic thinker, in commenting on the line stressed the fact that the "glass" in question was of course the *speculum,* or mirror, and that this world with its evil and perversity was a reversed mirror image of the heavenly realm. Again Borges places this comment of Bloy in a Gnostic framework and conjectures, "It is doubtful that the world has any sense; it's even more doubtful that it has double or triple sense. . . . I understand that that's the way it is; but I understand that the hieroglyphic world postulated by Bloy is the one that most suits the dignity of the intellectual God of the theologians" ("Es dudoso que el mundo tenga sentido; es más dudoso aún que tenga doble y triple sentido. . . . Yo entiendo que así es; pero entiendo que el mundo jeroglífico postulado por Bloy es el que más conviene a la dignidad del Dios intelectual de los teólogos").[62] Borges concludes that Bloy, though he considered himself to be a good Catholic, was like Swedenborg or Blake, really a heresiarch.

VII   *El hacedor*

Borges still writes an occasional note or commentary for a newspaper or for the magazine *Sur.* But his period of great essayistic productivity has apparently ended—unless, of course, in keeping with the cyclical pattern that he often observes in history, he will start writing essays once again. His age and blindness notwithstanding, Borges would be capable of doing just that. At any rate, one last group of compositions—the prose pieces of *El Hacedor* (1960)—must be noted before his best-known literary expression, his fiction, is discussed.

What are the prose compositions which make up the fifty-odd pages of *El hacedor?* An anthologist of Borges' work considers some of them "parables," [63] and another writer, a discerning critic says that they constitute an "exorcism" of "old, malignant spirits." [64] These pieces are, in many cases, the final reduction, the purest distillation of Borges' literary and intellectual world. As such, they do not lend themselves to further condensation or to easy résumés. In a word, they must be read to be appreciated. Most of them are presented in the first person, all simply and with a remarkable purity of style. The tone is one of gentle sincerity and decorum. With a few exceptions, *El hacedor* was composed during the period 1954–59, though many of the pieces have that quality of timelessness which Borges has always sought. The magnificent tribute to the blind Homer (*el hacedor*, the "maker" or "creator," par excellence) from which the collection takes its title, suggests without the slightest note of vanity, that the destinies of all creative men—Borges included—obliterate the vast distances of the centuries. On reading it we almost feel that Homer is Borges and that Borges is Homer. A different mood pervades the very personal "Dreamtigers," the title piece of the English version of *El hacedor*. In this piece we find the author confessing that in his dreams he is still the four-year-old child who sketched pictures of Indian tigers in his book of English nursery rhymes.[65] Some of the pieces are a mere dozen lines in length, others as long as two pages: a few of the twenty-four seem trivial, but many are deeply moving.

Whether or not Borges has in *El hacedor* really exorcised the spirits which have haunted, fascinated, inspired, amused, or bedeviled him throughout his life would be difficult to affirm or deny. Yet it seems that most of them, if not exorcised, are present as old friends rather than as malignant spirits: the once-feared mirrors, long-passed loves, Martín Fierro, Juan Facundo Quiroga, the transfigured face of Christ-Everyman, Macedonio Fernández, and perhaps the most haunting ghost of all, the Other Borges: "Years ago I tried to free myself from him and went from the mythologies of the suburbs to games with time and infinity, but those games belong to Borges now and I shall have to imagine other things. Thus my life is a flight and I lose everything, and everything belongs to oblivion, or to him. I do not know which of us has written this page" ("Hace años yo traté de librarme de él y pasé de las mitologías del arrabal a los juegos con el tiempo y con lo infinito, pero esos juegos son de Borges ahora y tendré que idear otras cosas. Así mi vida es una fuga y todo lo pierdo y todo es del olvido, o del otro. No sé cuál de los dos escribe esta página").[66]

CHAPTER 4

Borges the Writer of Fiction

THE line which divides Borges' essayistic prose from his fiction is an indistinct one. The book which is usually considered to mark this transition is his *Historia universal de la infamia* (1935). Rather than his first book of fiction, this collection of compositions is Borges' first prose work in which the narrative element dominates the expository. Only one piece, the "Hombre de la esquina rosada" ("The Man From The Rose-Colored Corner"), could properly be called a short story: the others are slightly fictionalized accounts of a curious group of ne'er-do-wells. The raw material for these sketches was drawn from literary or historical sources: the exception again is the "Hombre de la esquina rosada" whose material springs from the *barrio* folklore of Borges' childhood haunts, the Palermo district of Buenos Aires. Another piece which has strong narrative elements, "El acercamiento a Almotásim," ("The Approach to Almotasim") also occupies an indeterminate position between fiction and essay. First published in 1934, it appears both in the essay collection *Historia de la eternidad* and in the volume of short stories, *El jardín de senderos que se bifurcan*. "El acercamiento" has the form of a book review —but of a nonexistent book. This unusual framing device, understandably, has the effect of de-emphasizing the force of the narrative.

Borges approached fiction with considerable timidity. Significantly, the "Hombre de la esquina rosada" appeared first under a pseudonym, F. Bustos. And the prologue to the *Historia universal de la infamia* is almost apologetic in tone: the author explains that the pieces have no pretense of psychological validity and that they are mere "narratives" inspired by Stevenson, Chesterton, and Von Sternberg's gangster films. The fact of the matter is that Borges considered himself to be primarily a poet, secondarily an essayist, but certainly not a short story writer. Though fiction delighted him as a child and intrigued him as a young man, he had on several occasions expressed the idea that he viewed the genre as forbidden territory. Quite recently (1966) he made this point clear in a very revealing interview: "I was very timid, because when I was young I thought of myself as a poet. So I thought: 'If I write a story everybody will know I'm an outsider, that I am intruding in forbidden ground. . . .'"[1]

Borges tells us in a characteristically offhand manner that the title of this first narrrative collection, *Historia universal de la infamia,* is not to be taken very seriously: "the word *infamy* in the title is bewildering, but beneath all the tumult there is nothing" ("la palabra *infamia* aturde en el título, pero bajo los tumultos no hay nada").[2] And indeed there is not a great deal here except the charming, and often very funny, manner in which Borges retells the bizarre histories of his antiheroes: Lazarus Morrell, the "atrocious redeemer of slaves," who earned a tidy living by encouraging Negroes to flee their masters and then resold the escapees to other slaveholders; Tom Castro, a subequatorial confidence man who for many years deceived a comfortable widow by claiming to be her long-lost son; the Widow Ching, a completely incongruous cymbal-clashing, pirate queen of the China Seas; Monk Eastman, a New York mobster of the turn of the century who, after ten years in Sing Sing Prison and a military career, dies at the hands of an unknown assassin; the coldblooded Bill Harrigan—alias Billy the Kid—whose real and mythical exploits are well known to American readers; one Kotsuké No Suké, a samurai of ancient Japan, whose unforgettable person gives Borges the opportunity to explicate certain details of ancient Nippon's honor code; and finally Ha'kim de Merv, the mysterious and resplendent Veiled Prophet of Islamic lore who is ultimately revealed as a hideously deformed leper. Although these pieces are not "framed" as book reviews, Borges does inform the reader of his factual sources for most of the items—a further indication of his timidity, his desire to appear as a commentator, as a reteller of tales rather than as an original writer. In the "Hombre de la esquina rosada" by contrast, he mentions no specific literary sources or historical documentation. In it, he relates the story of a confrontation between two *compadritos* (neighborhood toughs of Buenos Aires slums of the late nineteenth century) who meet in a brothel, challenge each other, and fight. The piece is full of the *lunfardo* (typical Buenos

Aires slang), local color, and bravado that one might expect, given its theme and setting. While technically narrative fiction, it is more reminiscent of Borges' *criollista* poetry of the 1920's than it is of his major fiction.

Taken as a whole, the pieces of *Historia universal de la infamia* are, as Borges and his commentators agree, little more than exercises in narration. Yet a few characteristics typical of his later fiction do appear. Two of these are his use of the theme of the confrontation with destiny as seen in the duel of brave men ("El hombre de la esquina rosada"); and the tendency to present lives having no "symmetry," no poetic justice, but which simply end, prosaically and undramatically (Lazarus Morell, Tom Castro). Borges was, however, not quite ready to devote his full energies to this kind of writing. Significantly, between the publication of this collection, and the year 1939 he produced no prose fiction. He recalls that a few people seemed to have enjoyed his early attempts at narration and that he clearly did not consider fiction his *métier*.

Late in 1938 Borges suffered an accident which may have had a profound influence on his literary career. Returning to his apartment late one evening, he slipped on a poorly lit staircase and in falling was struck sharply on the head. For two weeks he remained hospitalized and in a serious condition. During this period he was plagued by insomnia, fever, and nightmares. While convalescing the fear that his mental powers and writing ability had suffered as a result of the accident constantly disturbed him. Since, as a writer of fiction he had no reputation nor personal standard to maintain, he chose to write some stories to see if his fears were justified. "I thought I would try my hand at writing an article or poem. But I thought: 'I have written hundreds of articles and poems. If I can't do it, then I'll know at once that I am done for . . .' So I thought I'd try my hand at something I hadn't done: if I couldn't do it, there would be nothing strange about it . . ." [3] The immediate result of this experiment was the story "Pierre Menard, autor del Quijote" which appeared in the spring of 1939 in *Sur*. About a year later "Tlön, Uqbar, Orbis Tertius" appeared, to be followed by the steady stream of "fictions" which has brought Borges the fame he now enjoys. The fact that his writing of short stories began with his period of convalescence has been stressed by Borges as well as by those who have written about him. But perhaps other factors should be considered in accounting for the appearance of his unique kind of fiction at this particular time. Those who condemn Borges' work frequently stress the essential "escapism" in much of his fiction, while sympathetic critics often suggest that the fantastic element in his work grows out of a desire to transcend the meaninglessness and horror of the world as it is. The defenders of both positions seem to agree at least on the fact that there is some relationship between the problems of the modern world and Borges' highly imaginative fiction. That such a relationship does exist is further indicated by the fact that the span of years covered by his production of fiction (1939–54) coincides almost exactly with some of the most unpleasant times that the world—and Argentina—have recently experienced. World War II, the Nazi's "final solution" of the "Jewish Problem," the rise of military dictatorship in Argentina and the Perón regime itself were events which unquestionably affected Borges deeply. Yet this kind of approach must not be carried too far: Borges has often stated that people take him much too seriously and that we would do well not to seek a hidden raison-d'être behind his work. One has the feeling that even if he had not injured himself on that fateful day late in 1938, and even if he had had the good fortune to live in happier times, he would still have written, sooner or later, something quite like the stories in *Ficciones, El Aleph,* and his other collections.

Borges' total production of prose fiction includes approximately fifty individual compositions. Ten of these pieces (those contained in the first edition of *Historia universal de la infamia,* and "El acercamiento de Almotásim") were written before 1939; the remainder, between that date and 1954. For bibliographic convenience they are grouped as stories, though some of these so-called stories are in fact essays. A number lie somewhere between the two genres, and perhaps should be considered as a distinct and unique literary form. Although Borges himself obviously puts little stock in strict generic divisions, for the sake of convenience, this portion of his literary production is best approached by analyzing first some representative pieces of "essayistic" fiction; secondly, several examples of his difficult-to-classify "intermediate" fiction; and finally, those compositions which may be considered conventional short stories.

I *Essayistic Fiction*

The phrase "essayistic fiction" may seem to be an unfortunate contradiction in terms, yet it is applicable to much of Borges' work. A representative sample of the pieces that could be placed under such a heading would include some of his most celebrated as well as some of his more deservedly ignored writings: "Funes el memorioso," "Pierre Menard, autor del Quijote," "Examen de la obra de Herbert Quain," "Tres versiones de Judas," and perhaps "El Zahir." These, and other pieces like them, are often based on readily identified philosophic notions, though many of the personalities used by Borges to make his points are fictional. In none of them is there any real narrative: several are based on invented literary notes describing fictitious authors and their works. It would not be difficult to imagine most of them cast in the form of the traditional essay.

"Funes el memorioso" recalls Borges' long-standing interest in problems of language and in the nature of memory. The central character, Ireneo Funes, is a lad of the Uruguayan pampas who, after a serious accident, becomes aware of the fact that he has a complete and photographic memory. Bits and pieces of his strange existence are described: how he calmly and effortlessly memorized the entire Latin text of Pliny's *Natural History;* how the complete causal train of events which stand behind any perceived object were known to him; how he attempted to organize and codify the vast storehouse of his memory, and how he suffered insomnia as a result of the myriads of precise impressions which crowded his mind. Borges uses the piece to digress on such arcane themes as the possibility of establishing an "infinite vocabulary" corresponding to the natural series of numbers, and Locke's project of devising "an impossible language in which each individual thing, each stone, each bird, and each branch, would have its own name . . ." ("un idioma imposible en el que cada cosa individual, cada piedra, cada pájaro, y cada rama tuviera un nombre propio . . .").[4] These themes are closely related to Borges' interest in nominalism and to his ideas on language as expressed in such essays as "Indagación de la palabra" and "El idioma analítico de John Wilkins." Though there is a note of horror in Funes's unusual gift—or curse—Borges emphasizes the intellectual content of the piece rather than the protagonist's personal destiny. Significantly, a single line describes the end of Funes's shadowy existence: "Ireneo Funes died in 1889, of congestion of the lungs" ("Ireneo Funes murió en 1889, de una congestión pulmonar").[5] Of greater importance, perhaps, is Borges' comment on the relationship of memory and forgetting to the nature of understanding: "With no effort he had learned English, French, Portuguese and Latin. I suspect, however, that he was not very capable of thought. To think is to forget differences, generalize, make abstractions. In the teeming world of Funes, there were only details, almost immediate in their presence" ("Había aprendido sin esfuerzo el inglés, el francés, el portugués, el latín. Sospecho, sin embargo que no era muy capaz de pensar. Pensar es olvidar diferencias, es generalizar, abstraer. En el abarrotado mundo de Funes no había sino detalles, casi inmediatos").[6]

"Pierre Menard, autor del Quijote" is another one of the better known pieces which serves to illustrate Borgesian essayistic fiction. It is also a fine example of Borges' humor, a facet of his literary personality too frequently ignored. The title of the piece first arouses curiosity; later it produces a wry, philosophic smile—especially if the reader happens to be an academic. The piece seems to be clipped from the pages of a somewhat old-fashioned scholarly journal. Writing in the first person, Borges affects the tone of a pretentious academic hack: his first task is to rectify certain unpardonable omissions "perpetrated" by another—and obviously less competent—student of Menard's work. After a paragraph of charmingly pompous name-dropping, the author presents a two-page bibliography of Menard's publications. Though completely apocryphal, the works listed show much internal consistency, bookish humor, and gentle ironies. To appreciate fully Menard's far-ranging interests (chess, seventeenth- and eighteenth-century philosophy, French Symbolism, and Paul Valéry) one must be a bit of an expert on these subjects, and on Borges as well. Not only does the author give us an enumeration of Menard's publications, but he even includes dates, footnotes, and the names of real journals in which he supposedly wrote. But all this is a mere preliminary. The main part of the piece describes Menard's writing of the *Quijote:* not just "another *Quijote* . . . but *the Quijote itself!*" ("No quería componer otro *Quijote* . . .

sino *el Quijote*").[7] As Borges reports Menard's expression of this
modest desire, "My intent is no more than astonishing" ("Mi
propósito es meramente asombroso").[8]

Menard first thinks of immersing himself in the world of Cervantes; of learning Spanish, of fighting the Moors, of recovering
his lost Catholic faith, and of forgetting all the post-Cervantine
history that he had ever learned. Realizing the impossibility of
this approach, he concludes that he would go on being simply
Pierre Menard and would attempt, in some manner, to reach the
Quijote through his own experiences. When pressed to explain
why he chose Cervantes' book over any other for this remarkable
tour de force, Menard explains (with impressively specious logic)
that the *Don Quijote* was philosophically a "contingent" or unnecessary work. Hence, one could write it in a premeditated manner,
"without falling into a tautology" ("sin incurrir en una
tautología").[9] By contrast, certain other literary masterpieces,
Poe's poetry, for example, would not lend themselves to such a
project since they are logically "necessary." After all, Menard reasons, "Poe . . . engendered Baudelaire, who engendered Mallarmé, who engendered Valéry, who engendered Edward Teste"
("Poe . . . engendró a Baudelaire, que engendró a Mallarmé,
que engendró a Valéry, que engendró a Edmond Teste").[10]

At any rate, Menard writes his *Quijote* and Borges undertakes a
close textual comparison of Cervantes' work with that of the
Frenchman's. The two texts, we are told, "are verbally identical,
but the second is almost infinitely richer" ("Son verbalmente idén-
ticos, pero el segundo es casi infinitamente más rico").[11] Borges—
half tongue-in-cheek—also points out that Menard's *Quijote* is
more subtle and more ambitious than Cervantes' effort. After all,
wasn't Menard a contemporary of William James and Bertrand
Russell? And isn't Nietzschean influence clearly evident in his
work? In the last few pages Menard's hazy existence is almost
completely obscured by the provocative essayistic digressions
which Borges introduces. He concludes the piece with the thought
that "Menard (perhaps without wanting to) has enriched, by
means of a new technique, the halting and rudimentary art of
reading: this new technique is that of the deliberate anachronism
and the erroneous attribution" ("Menard [acaso sin quererlo] ha
enriquecido mediante una técnica nueva el arte detenido y rudi-
mentario de la lectura: la técnica del anacronismo deliberado y de

las atribuciones erróneas").[12] Finally, he suggests some possible applications of the technique: for example, why not attribute the *Imitation of Christ* to James Joyce, or why not consider the *Odyssey* as coming after the *Aeneid?* "Pierre Menard, autor del Quijote" will strike those who are well grounded in literature, literary criticism—and Borges—as clever, sophisticated, and quite funny. Others may find it dull, obscurely bookish, and quite pointless. The first group of readers will enjoy Borges' feigned pomposity, the "inside" jokes, the caricature of the literary world's petty feuds. They may also see a not-too-implausible reflection of Borges himself in Pierre Menard. Certainly the underlying ideas regarding the flow of time, authorship, plagiarism, and the philosophic interest in the contingent versus the necessary are Borges' as well as Menard's. Occasionally, an offhand remark describing Menard's personal or literary quirks have a remarkably introspective ring. When, for example, Borges points out Menard's "resigned or ironical habit of propagating ideas which were the strict reverse of those he preferred" ("su hábito resignado o irónico de propagar ideas que eran el estricto reverso de las preferidas por él"),[13] one thinks of Borges himself. We are even more likely to make this association when Borges writes that Menard "decided to anticipate the vanity awaiting all man's efforts; he set himself to an undertaking which was exceedingly complex and from the very beginning, futile" ("Resolvió adelantarse a la vanidad que aguarda todas las fatigas del hombre; acometió una empresa complejísima y de antemano fútil").[14]

Several other pieces, though not as well known as either "Funes" or "Pierre Menard," illustrate additional facets of Borges' essayistic fiction. The central character of "Un examen de la obra de Herbert Quain" is a kind of English Pierre Menard. He is, of course, fictional; but the literary environment in which he moves is quite real: references to English and American authors (Agatha Christie, Bulwer Lytton, F. H. Bradley, and others) are sprinkled throughout and mention of noted publications such as the *Times Literary Supplement,* recalls the insertion of real publications in Pierre Menard's fake bibliography. Quain's remarkable literary experiment was, however, quite different from Menard's and probably less demanding. This celebrated—and apocryphal—author of detective fiction proposed and successfully produced a "branching, regressive novel," titled appropriately *April March.*

Borges describes the work in some detail. The time line runs backward: that is, a scar precedes a wound as death precedes birth; and, most important, after the first chapter, the plot divides into three plots, each of which in turn splits into three other plots. In short, the reader of *April March* may choose to read any one of nine distinct novels. Moreover, Borges slyly writes, these provide the reader with the choice of reading (in the same book) novels which may be described as "symbolic, supernatural, detective, psychological, communist, anticommunist, etc." ("... de carácter simbólico ... supernatural ... policial ... psicológico ... comunista ... anticomunista, etcétera").[15] To clarify this strange device, Borges even diagrams the book's structure with the comment that others, no doubt, will imitate it using a binary system or perhaps even one involving infinite ramifications.

In the remainder of the piece Borges describes some of Quain's other bizarre literary games: a complex and unlikely "Freudian comedy" and a collection of eight tales the plots of which have been deliberately truncated for the use of "imperfect writers" who may wish to complete them. "Un examen de la obra de Herbert Quain," like "Pierre Menard, autor del Quijote," lacks any real narrative: it is a witty, literary *divertimento* which could have been written as an essay, though the vehicle which Borges chose to use certainly enhances its total effect, especially its humor. In this piece Borges practices the kind of literary gamesmanship which many have praised and a few have condemned. What he writes of Quain's novel could easily be written of Borges' own work: "No one, upon judging this novel, denies that it is a game; it is well to recall that its author never considered it anything but that. 'I claim for this work,' I once heard him remark, 'The essential characteristics of all games: symmetry, arbitrary rules, [and] tedium'" ("Nadie, al juzgar esa novela, se niega a descubrir que es un juego; es lícito recordar que el autor no la consideró nunca otra cosa. *Yo reivindico para esa obra*, le oí decir, *los rasgos esenciales de todo juego: la simetría, las leyes arbitrarias, el tedio*").[16] Aside from the game of presenting a self-caricature Borges compounds the literary joke by citing in the works of the fictitious Quain, the sources of two of his own stories, "Las ruinas circulares" and "El jardín de senderos que se bifurcan."

Like Pierre Menard and Herbert Quain, Nils Runeberg's life and works are products of Borges' imagination. The protagonist of

"Tres versiones de Judas," Runeberg is a Protestant theologian of the early twentieth century. The atmosphere in which he moves is one of Scandinavian seriousness, of ponderous scholarship centered about christological mysteries and haunted perhaps by the ghosts of Swedenborg and Kierkegaard. Borges states at the outset that Runeberg would have been happier in second-century Alexandria, in the world of Basilides and other Gnostic heresiarchs. Runeberg's all-consuming scholarly passion is the study of the problems posed by Judas' betrayal of Christ. In some three pages of heavily documented prose, Borges outlines the theologian's preliminary theories, his arguments with other scholars, real and fictional, and his final position on the relationship between Judas and Christ: "God made Himself totally a man but a man to the point of infamy, a man to the point of reprobation and the abyss. To save us He could have chosen any of the destinies which make up the complex web of history; He could have been Alexander or Pythagoras or Rurik or Jesus; He chose the vilest destiny of all: He was Judas" ("Dios totalmente se hizo hombre pero hombre hasta la infamia, hombre hasta la reprobación y el abismo. Para salvarnos, pudo elegir cualquiera de los destinos que traman la perpleja red de la historia; pudo ser Alejandro o Pitágoras o Rurik o Jesús; eligió un ínfimo destino: fué Judas").[17] Borges remarks quite casually that the bookstores had a difficult time selling Runeberg's masterpiece and that from then on his protagonist, "drunk with insomnia and vertiginous dialectic" ("Ebrio de insomnio y de vertiginosa dialéctica"),[18] led a rather isolated life, somewhat out of touch with the academic community, if not with the world at large. In typical Borgesian fashion, Runeberg's final destiny is reported in matter-of-fact terms: "He died of a ruptured aneurysm on the first of March, 1912" ("Murió de la rotura de un aneurisma, el primero de marzo de 1912").[19]

The subject matter of the "Tres versiones de Judas" is familiar to the readers of Borges' nonfictional prose. His essays of the early 1930's, "Vindicación del falso Basilides" and "Vindicación de la Cábala," it will be recalled, dealt directly with Gnosticism and especially with the idea of "inverting" the values and heroes of the main Judeo-Christian tradition. That Cain might be the "good" brother, that Satan might be the more legitimate representative of the Creator, or that Judas rather than Jesus might be the Son of God are notions quite amenable to the Gnostic heresies. Borges, of course, is neither a theologian nor an especially religious man. His attitude in the "Tres versiones de Judas" is one of mild amusement; mitigated, no doubt, by a respectful admiration for his fictional creation, and for others like him who divulge "terrible secrets" and propose superbly reasoned blasphemies. The essayistic character of this piece is underscored by the abundant documentation and by the lack of any real narrative save the rather dry details of Runeberg's scholarly career. Borges even includes several rambling footnotes in mock academic style. In one of these, he again plays a favorite literary game by referring to Jaromir Hladík and his book *Vindication of Eternity:* the reference, buried amidst the names of several real writers, is to a fictional creation of Borges, the protagonist of the story "El milagro secreto."

II   *Intermediate Fiction*

The foregoing pieces, while they do not include all of Borges' essayistic fiction, should serve to illustrate this facet of his imaginative prose. A great deal of his work nonetheless falls into an intermediate category which incorporates features of his essayistic fiction as well as of the genuine short story. These compositions are perhaps the most difficult of any to analyze and evaluate; yet they include some of his most discussed pieces and ones which are, for many, the most "typically Borgesian." Our survey of this group of Borges' compositions may begin by an examination of "Tlön, Uqbar, Orbis Tertius," a work whose title alone is sufficient to frighten away the fainthearted and confuse the uninitiated.

One of his longer *Ficciones,* "Tlön, Uqbar, Orbis Tertius," is a tour de force of literary gamesmanship, of playful philosophizing, of linguistic dabbling and of urbane humor. Yet the piece retains an essential seriousness which only becomes evident in its closing pages. Written by a less talented author it might have been organized as a conventional essay; another writer might have begun by saying "Let us posit the existence of an imaginary universe in which the basic tenets of Berkeley's idealism have been accepted as the fundamental world view: let us further state that the language, science, history and literature of this world all flow from the implications of this philosophical position, and that what we think of as common-sense realism and science based on simple empirical observations, are, to the inhabitants of our imagined universe, highly questionable if not heretical doctrines." Borges in effect says something quite similar to this in the story, but his statement appears only after the reader has navigated through some seven pages of highly unusual, and even for those familiar with Borges, highly confusing material.

"Tlön, Uqbar, Orbis Tertius" is presented in a chatty first-person style. The author begins by telling how one evening his very real friend, Bioy Casares, happened to make a casual reference to a religious writer of Uqbar. When Borges confessed that he was unfamiliar with both the writer and the land of Uqbar, Bioy replied that his information came from *The Anglo-American Cyclopedia,* a set of which just happened to have been in the house Borges had recently rented. However, on examining the encyclopedia (a "delinquent pirating" of the tenth edition of the *Britannica,* Borges notes parenthetically) they find no article on Uqbar. Dismayed and confused, they agree that it must exist somewhere in either the Near or Middle East. The next day Bioy calls Borges to inform him that he had located a copy of the encyclopedia which did indeed contain the piece on Uqbar. On careful examination of the particular volume they find that Borges' copy contained only 917 pages, while Bioy's had 921—the four extra pages being those describing Uqbar. The article itself, characterized by "rigorous prose" beneath which was "a fundamental vagueness," gave no concrete statement regarding Uqbar's exact location. Further checking, in such standard works as Perthe's atlas and Ritter's geography, revealed nothing whatever about this mysterious land.

The riddle of Uqbar is left unsolved, and the events described in the second section of the story take place two years afterward. At this point Borges relates, in minute detail, how he came into possession of an even more mysterious work, a single volume of *A First Encyclopedia of Tlön* (Vol. XI Hlaer to Jangr). It seems that a certain Herbert Ashe, an eccentric English railway engineer and an acquaintance of Borges' father, had been mailed a book from a mysterious friend—a vaguely identified Norwegian, living in Brazil, no less. Ashe, however, died (oddly enough, like Nils Runeberg of a "ruptured aneurysm") shortly before the package arrived at the hotel in Adrogué where the Borges family frequently stayed. In this manner the mysterious parcel containing the book came into Borges' possession. The only reference to

Uqbar occurs when he remarks "Two years before I had discovered, in a volume of a certain pirated encyclopedia, a superficial description of a nonexistent country; now chance offered me something more precious and arduous" ("Hacía dos años que yo había descubierto en un tomo de cierta enciclopedia pirática una somera descripción de un falso país; ahora me deparaba el azar algo más precioso y más arduo").[20]

Though only one tome of the *Encyclopedia of Tlön* could be located—even after such worthies as Alfonso Reyes, Ezequiel Martínez Estrada, and Nestor Ibarra,[21] help in the search for companion volumes—Borges finds enough material in the book to sketch out certain basic features of Tlönian culture. After explaining the "congenital idealism" of the planet, Borges discusses Tlön's languages in some detail. Since the Tlönian's basic world view denies the existence of objects in space, there are no nouns in their languages; instead "there are impersonal verbs, modified by monosyllabic suffixes (or prefixes) with an adverbial value" ("hay verbos impersonales, calificados por sufijos o prefijos monosilábicos de valor adverbial").[22] Thus, Borges explains, they have no substantive for "moon," but a verb which should be "to moon" ("lunar") or "to moonate" ("lunecer") hence the sentence, "The moon rose above the river" ("Surgió la luna sobre el río") is *hlör u fang axaxaxas mlö*, or literally "upward behind the onstreaming it mooned" ("hacia arriba detrás duradero-fluir lunecío").[23] Tlönian science—what there is of it—is dominated by the planet's "classical" discipline, psychology. Since Tlönians have no conception of objects in space persisting in time, our notion of causality is nonexistent: "The perception of a cloud of smoke on the horizon and then of a burning field and then of the half-extinguished cigarette that produced the blaze is considered an example of the association of ideas" ("La percepción de una humareda en el horizonte y después del campo incendiado y después del cigarro a medio apagar que produjo la quemazón es considerada un ejemplo de asociación de ideas").[24] Moreover, Borges tells us that on Tlön every mental state is "irreducible"; hence the idea of classification suggests falsification and as a result "there are no sciences on Tlön, not even reasoning" ("no hay ciencias en Tlön— ni siquiera razonamientos").[25] Yet in a sense, there are sciences on Tlön, but such an infinitude of scientific systems exists that they are better thought of as individual "dialectical games." Neither

Tlön's "scientists" nor her metaphysicians seek truth as we understand the term. Instead they seek "astounding" theories; as Borges puts it, the Tlönians have "an abundance of incredible systems of pleasing design or sensational type" ("Abundan los sistemas increíbles, pero de arquitectura agradable o de tipo sensacional").[26] A few misguided individuals insist on materialism, and on systems which rest upon our usual notions of cause and effect. In a series of amusingly inverted paradoxes—too lengthy to be discussed here—Borges shows how Tlön's more sober minds have refuted these heresies.

Borges' analysis of Tlönian literary theories and practices is rich in self-caricature. We are informed that on Tlön books are not usually signed, for the idea "that all works are the creation of one author, who is atemporal and anonymous" ("que todas las obras son obra de un solo autor, que es intemporal y es anónimo") seems to dominate literary attitudes. Plagiarism, is, of course, a meaningless concept. "The critics often invent authors: they select two dissimilar works—the *Tao Te Ching* and the *Thousand and One Nights,* say—attribute them to the same writer and then determine most scrupulously the psychology of this interesting *homme de lettres* . . ." ("La crítica suele inventar autores: elige dos obras disímiles—el Tao Te Ching y las 1001 Noches, digamos—, las atribuye a un mismo escritor y luego determina con probidad la psicología de ese interesante *homme de lettres* . . .").[27] Borges also notes that a favorite device in Tlönian fiction is the use of a single plot, but arranged in all its possible permutations.

Perhaps the most curious Tlönian phenomenon is the appearance of *hrönir;* that is, objects which are produced by various kinds of mental activity. As Borges blandly notes, "Centuries and centuries of idealism have not failed to influence reality" ("Siglos y siglos de idealismo no han dejado de influir en la realidad").[28] At first merely "accidental products" of distraction and forgetfulness, the *hrönir* were later deliberately produced. Thus Tlönian archeologists who wish to prove a point simply *think* the necessary artifacts into existence: "The methodical fabrication of *hrönir* . . . has made possible the interrogation and even the modification of the past, which is now no less plastic and docile than the future" ("La metódica elaboración de *hrönir* . . . Ha permitido interrogar y hasta modificar el pasado, que ahora no es menos plástico y menos dócil que el porvenir").[29] Finally, Borges indulges himself in a rather prolix discussion of how there are *hrönir* of *hrönir,* and of how these duplicates of duplicates may exist in an infinite series, although with a certain pattern of periodicity.

At this point the story of Tlön abruptly ends with Borges giving us the date of composition (1940) and the place in which he had written the piece (Salto Oriental). But the show is not really over. A lengthy "Postscript," dated 1947, follows. Readers of recent editions of "Tlön, Uqbar, Orbis Tertius" in all probability would not question the date of the "Postscript." However, they would then be victims of one of Borges' frequent literary jokes; for the entire 1947 addition was written in 1940 and appeared as part of the original story as published in the May issue of the magazine *Sur.* It is clear that Borges' efforts to "refute" time are not limited to mere essays on the subject!

The so-called Postscript is devoted to a lengthy explanation of events and discoveries which supposedly take place between 1941 and 1944, and which shed light on the true authors of the *Encyclopedia of Tlön.* It seems that a seventeenth-century secret society dedicated to hermetic studies and the Kabala, decided to "invent" a country. Although the original members of the group failed to carry out this objective, the society and their plan persisted: after a few centuries it sprang up again in the ante-bellum South of the United States. One Ezra Buckley, an eccentric millionaire of Memphis, Tennessee, whom Borges slyly describes in a footnote as a "freethinker, a fatalist, and a defender of slavery" ("libre pensador, fatalista y defensor de la esclavitud"), becomes the patron of the resuscitated society. Buckley, who could easily have stepped out of the pages of the *Historia universal de la infamia,* was apparently given to Gnostic heresies: he agrees to subvent the society's preparation of a forty-volume encyclopedia of the fictional planet, provided "The work will make no pact with the imposter Jesus Christ" ("La obra no pactará con el impostor Jesucristo").[30] Evidently these terms were accepted, for many years after Buckley's demise (we are told, with no further explanation, that he was poisoned in 1828) the secret printing of the *Encyclopedia* was distributed to the society's members. Years later, through the same Herbert Ashe, whom we had met earlier, a single volume falls into Borges' possession. Finally, Borges reports, in 1944 a complete forty-volume collection is discovered in the Memphis, Tennessee, public library! The discovery of the *En-*

cyclopedia's origin would seem to resolve all of the questions which surrounded the apocryphal world of Tlön. But while Borges drops this veil of mystery he raises another. Inexplicable objects— a strangely heavy metal cone, a compass marked with the symbols of Tlön's alphabet—begin to appear. In short, a fantastic world intrudes upon our world of reality. Though Borges' tale bears some resemblance to such popular genres as fantasy and science fiction, his narrative never quite becomes typical of these literary forms. Despite such old-hat devices as having dreamt or imagined objects impinge on the real world, his work differs from these genres in that it is richer in literary allusions and in sophisticated ironies. There is, moreover, an underlying seriousness which pervades much of the story.

This tone of seriousness is especially evident in the final paragraphs of "Tlön, Uqbar, Orbis Tertius." Borges notes that the world, on learning of Tlön and upon receiving the "corroborating" evidence of the strange objects noted above, seemed all too willing to "yield" reality to the attractive symmetry of this well-ordered planet: "The truth is that it longed to yield. Ten years ago any symmetry with a semblance of order—dialectical materialism, anti-Semitism, Naziism—was sufficient to entrance the minds of men. How could one do other than submit to Tlön, to the minute and vast evidence of an orderly planet?" ("Lo cierto es que anhelaba ceder. Hace diez años bastaba cualquier simetría con apariencia de orden—el materialismo dialéctico, el antisemitismo, el nazismo—para embelesar a los hombres. ¿Cómo no someterse a Tlön, a la minuciosa y vasta evidencia de un planeta ordenado?").[31] At the tale's conclusion Borges, writing in the first person, finds the world as he has known it slipping away: history is being rewritten, language is being transformed by the "conjectural, primitive" idiom of Tlön, and all fields of learning will soon be profoundly altered. In short, "The world will be Tlön" ("El mundo será Tlön"). Despite the uncertainties of what is about to take place, Borges writes, "I pay no attention to all this and go on revising . . . an uncertain Quevedian translation (which I do not intend to publish) of Browne's *Urn Burial*." ("Yo no hago caso, yo sigo revisando . . . una indecisa traducción quevediana [que no pienso dar a la imprenta] del *Urn Burial* de Browne").[32]

In retrospect, "Tlön, Uqbar, Orbis Tertius" almost defies description. Although it is hardly a short story by the usual stand-

ards of the genre, the author's persistent tracking down of the
"facts" surrounding Uqbar and later Tlön, does give it a narrative
tension more typical of this genre than of the essay. The excruciating amount of documentary detail (half real, half fictitious) may,
by contrast, make the piece seem more like an essay. Yet the mood
of the final pages, the picture of the author steadily and deliberately working away at his literary tasks while the world is slowly
being infected by Tlön's symmetrical madness, lends the piece a
personal dimension which Borges' "essayistic fiction" usually lacks.

In the prologue to his *Ficciones* Borges writes that "The composition of vast books is an exhausting and laborious nonsense . . ."
("Desvarío laborioso y empobrecedor el de componer vastos libros . . .").[33] After all, he reasons, why expend the effort to write
a five-hundred-page volume when the central idea of most books
can be stated orally in a few minutes: "A better procedure is to
make believe that the books already exist and offer a résumé, a
commentary" ("Mejor procedimiento es simular que esos libros ya
existen y ofrecer un resumen, un comentario"). Compared with
the world's great novelists, Borges confesses that he is "more sensible, more lazy, and more inept," and so he prefers "writing notes
on imaginary books" ("la escritura de notas sobre libros imagi-
narios").[34] In the very early "Acercamiento a Almotásim" he follows this plan perhaps more closely than in either "Pierre Menard,
autor del Quijote" or "Un examen de la obra de Herbert Quain,"
pieces to which it bears some structural similarity. Moreover, "Almotásim" differs from these compositions, so much so, that the
reader follows the story line of this nonexistent, half-allegorical,
half-detective novel with considerable interest. For this reason,
"Almotásim," despite the fact that it first appeared in a collection
of essays, is closer to a genuine short story than either "Menard"
or "Quain."

Borges begins by citing the real English writer, Phillip Guedalla, who supposedly has written a review of the nonexistent *Approach to Al-Mu'tasim* whose equally nonexistent author is one
Mir Bahadur Ali, a Bombay lawyer. Guedalla and others agree
that the book in question employs the mechanical devices of detective fiction with a "mystic undercurrent." After giving a few
details concerning the various editions of the work, Borges describes the main features of the novel's plot: A young law student
of Bombay gets involved in a riot between Moslems and Hindus;

he has probably killed someone in the confusion and is chased to a rooftop where he meets a "squalid" wretch of a man who is a professional corpse robber. The following morning the robber is gone and the protagonist decides to flee the city in search of a certain "woman of the thief's caste" whom his companion had mentioned. A long period of wandering follows during which the protagonist lives among the vilest of India's criminal class committing the most infamous of crimes imaginable. One day, however, he notices in one of his unsavory companions "a certain mitigation in this infamy: a tenderness, an exaltation . . ." ("alguna mitigación de esa infamia: una ternura, una exaltación . . ."). The protagonist realizes that this person was himself incapable of this tenderness; he concludes that this "mitigation" of the man's profound badness could only be a "reflection" of the good in another, or perhaps a reflection of a reflection. He reasons that "somewhere on earth there is a man from whom this clarity emanates; somewhere on earth there is a man who is like this clarity" ("En algún punto de la tierra hay un hombre de quien procede esa claridad; en algún punto de la tierra esta el hombre que es igual a esa claridad").[35] The balance of the fictitious book is devoted to the hero's ascending search for this pure being, whom we learn is "the man called Almotásim." After many years of seeking him, the law student finally gets to Almotásim's immediate antecedent, an unnamed Persian bookseller. Our hero is told that just beyond a certain door he will find Almotásim. He knocks upon the indicated door, "the incredible voice" of Almotásim tells him to enter, and as he opens it, Bahadur's novel—and Borges' retelling of it—end.

But Borges does not end the piece at this point. Instead he explains how the second edition of the novel "breaks down into allegory"; how Almotásim becomes an obvious "emblem" of God; and how the hero's quest becomes a rather typical metaphor of the soul's mystic ascent. Unstimulated by all this, Borges suggests the possibility that Almotásim, whose name, we are told, means "the seeker of shelter," may also be seeking "Another." The idea of one god in search of another god, in turn searching for another, of course appeals greatly to Borges: it gives him the opportunity to present one more example of his cherished infinite series. Were it not for this digression, and for the rather lengthy concluding discussion of remote literary sources, echoes, and affinities, the piece,

its unusual framing device notwithstanding, might have been
more like a traditional short story. As it stands, however, "El acercamiento de Almotásim" lies about midway between the essayistic
narratives and the true short story and is best thought of as an
example of Borges' intermediate fiction.

"El Aleph" and "El Zahir" occupy similar positions in this
spectrum, yet they are not quite like the piece just considered.
Although Borges states that both were suggested by H. G. Wells's
story "The Crystal Egg," they are not presented as *marginalia* to
nonexistent books. Of the two, "El Aleph" is the more interesting,
perhaps because it is, at least the writer's opinion, one of
Borges' funniest pieces. Yet some critics have ignored its humor,
and instead have attacked the piece as an excellent example of
Borges' worst literary sins.[36] Of interest, too, is the fact that some
of the humor in "El Aleph" is related to specific events in Borges'
career, namely, his not winning the National Prize for Literature
in 1942.

In the first half of the story Borges develops a delightful vi-
gnette of one of the very few characters in his fiction who enjoys
the double distinction of being thoroughly antipathetic and yet
who is taken seriously. Most of the villains and ne'er-do-wells
which appear in Borges' work hardly disturb their author or his
readers. They are typically too literary, too remote, or just too
unbelievable. Not so in the case of Carlos Argentino Daneri, a
contemporary *porteño*, full of literary pretensions, verbose, and a
complete bore. A man whose mental activity, writes Borges, "is
continuous, passionate, versatile, and completely insignificant" ("es
continua, apasionada, versátil, y del todo insignificante").[37] For
several pages Daneri annoys Borges by showing him selections of
his verse—dreadful bits of doggerel from his epic description
of the planet, modestly titled "La tierra." After each example of
verse Borges is forced to listen to a long-winded justification of
the particular selection: "I realized that the poet's work was not in
the poetry; it was in the invention of reasons by which it would be
considered admirable . . ." ("Comprendí que el trabajo del
poeta no estaba en la poesía; estaba en la invención de razones
para que la poesía fuera admirable . . .").[38] In view of Borges'
verbal sensitivity, the fact that this half-baked literary buffoon
should be named Carlos *Argentino* Daneri, cannot be attributed
to chance. Clearly Carlos is a caricature of some of the rather

stupid, but nonetheless influential, members of Argentina's literary establishment. Even though "El Aleph" was written in 1945, it is quite possible that when Borges created Carlos Argentino he had in mind some of the jury that denied him recognition in 1942. Support for this interpretation is found in the "postscript" to the story. Dated March, 1943 (a date which, incidentally, is questionable, since "El Aleph" appeared first in 1945) this addendum explains how Carlos' magnificent literary efforts were crowned with the second National Prize for Literature while Borges' own "Los naipes del Tahur" ("The Gambler's Deck") (a nonexistent work, of course) did not even figure in the voting!

But "El Aleph" is not simply a character sketch of Carlos Argentino Daneri, though his ludicrous figure dominates the mood of the tale more than it might first seem. The narrative—what there is of one—really begins when Borges receives a frantic telephone call from Argentino. It seems that the venerable house of his parents and grandparents is about to be demolished and with it, a priceless treasure. Argentino explains that in the basement of the house there is "an Aleph," without which he could not possibly write his monumental epic poem. Argentino further explains that "an Aleph is one of the points in space that contains all of the points" ("un Aleph es uno de los puntos del espacio que contienen todos los puntos").[39] Borges still doesn't quite understand, and so Argentino tells how he found it as a child, how it belongs to him, and how everything in the world is contained within it. Borges, his confusion compounded, decides to visit the house with Carlos to see for himself just what an "Aleph" might be. With Argentino as his guide, Borges descends the basement stairs, meticulously arranges himself and various objects according to the instructions of Argentino (whom he now fears may be a homicidal maniac), closes his eyes and then opens them.

At this point he sees the Aleph. Yet he complains "here begins my desperation as a writer . . . how to transmit to others the infinite Aleph, which my frightened memory can hardly contain?" ("empieza, aquí, mi desesperación de escritor . . . ¿cómo transmitir a los otros el infinito Aleph, que mi temerosa memoria apenas abarca?").[40] He recalls that one ancient sage described this mystic point-which-is-all-points as "a sphere whose center is everywhere and whose circumference is nowhere" ("una esfera cuyo centro está en todas partes y la circunferencia en ninguna"),[41] while other writers used different images. At any rate, despite the problems involved, Borges attempts a direct—and perhaps tongue-in-cheek—description of the Aleph and what he experienced by virtue of it: "On the lower part of the stairway, towards the right, I saw a small irridescent sphere of almost unbearable brilliance. At first I thought it was revolving; later I learned that this movement was an illusion. . . . The diameter of the Aleph was about two or three centimeters, but cosmic space was there without any decrease in size" ("En la parte inferior del escalón, hacia la derecha, vi una pequeña esfera tornasolada, de casi intolerable fulgor. Al principio la creí giratoria; luego comprendí que ese movimiento era una ilusión. . . . El diámetro del Aleph sería de dos o tres centímetros, pero el espacio cósmico estaba ahí, sin disminución de tamaño").[42] Borges then devotes almost two pages to a fantastic enumeration of all that he saw in the Aleph. Among the infinitude of items are included "all the mirrors of the world and all without my reflection" ("todos los espejos del planeta y ninguno me reflejó"); "a silvery spiderweb in the center of a dark pyramid" ("una plateada telaraña en el centro de una negra pirámide"); "all the ants in the world" ("todas las hormigas que hay en la tierra"); "a beach along the Caspian Sea" ("una playa del Mar Caspio"); bisons; tigers; obscene letters; and so on. In short, Borges remarks, he saw "the inconceivable universe" ("el inconcebible universo") and felt "infinite veneration, infinite sorrow" ("infinita veneración, infinita lástima").[43] At this dramatic moment he hears "a jovial and hateful voice": friend Argentino, calling from the top of cellar stairs is inquiring if "Che Borges" enjoyed the spectacle and if he saw everything in color!

The contrast between the mystery and wonder of the Aleph's revelation and Argentino's banal comment is perhaps the most effective part of the story. More important, it serves to define the piece as essentially humorous rather than terribly philosophical. Borges often complains that he is taken too seriously: when writers criticize a story such as "El Aleph" on the ground that the fantastic elements in the piece are presented in an awkward or inept manner, they do precisely what Borges objects to. Taken as a serious example of fantastic fiction or as a solemn exposition of the mystical notion of the identity between the macrocosm and microcosm (a theme touched upon by Borges frequently, as in his essay "La esfera de Pascal" or in the tale "El espejo de tinta"

["The Ink Mirror"]), the piece falls flat. Taken as a half-philosophical, basically playful composition—generously sprinkled with Borgesian irony and satire—"El Aleph" comes off rather well.

"El Zahir" is similar to the preceding tale in several ways: written in the first person, it presents the unlikely situation of a bit of oriental hocus-pocus intruding upon the author's workaday existence in contemporary Buenos Aires. As in "El Aleph," Borges develops a simple narrative full of specific and often prosaic detail against which the fantastic element stands in sharp contrast. The "Zahir" itself is any object—in this case a coin that the author picks up as change in a bar—which possesses "the terrible property of being unforgettable, and whose image finally drives one mad" ("la terrible virtud de ser inolvidable y cuya imagen acaba por enloquecer a la gente").[44] Though haunted by the vision of this ordinary coin, at first Borges does not realize just what has happened. He finally discovers a book in which the Zahir is explained at great length. This discovery provides the necessary crevice in the narrative in which to insert a substantial and very erudite discussion of the subject. But knowledge of the Zahir does not liberate the author from its pernicious influence: at night he is plagued by insomnia or by fitful sleep during which he has nightmarish dreams of the Zahir, and by day the image of anything which is not the Zahir becomes fragmentary or distorted. He visits a psychiatrist; he hears stories about others who have had the same malady; finally he becomes certain that he is going mad, that he will soon have to be spoon-fed and dressed. He even ponders the thought that others will be infected by the Zahir—perhaps even the whole world: "When all the men on earth think day and night of the Zahir, which will be a dream and which a reality—the earth or the Zahir?" ("Cuando todos los hombres de la tierra piensen, día y noche, en el Zahir ¿cuál será un sueño y cuál una realidad, la tierra o el Zahir?").[45]

The word *Zahir*, we are told, in Arabic means "notorious" or "visible." It is considered, moreover, to be one of the ninety-nine names of God in Islamic lore. Borges cites authors who describe it as a tiger, as an astrolabe, a piece of marble, a rose, or the "Shadow of the Rose." Borges further suggests that under the spell of the Zahir, one's view of the world takes on a spherical shape and that an infinitude of objects are superimposed on the field of vision. The similarity with the basic idea of "El Aleph" is of course obvious here. This microcosm-macrocosm identity is reinforced by references to the Kabalists, to certain ideas of Schopenhauer and to Tennyson's notion that if we could understand a single flower, we would understand ourselves and the entire universe. On balance, however, "El Zahir" suffers from too much essayistic material and from a somewhat unconvincing portrayal of the author's inpending madness: it cannot quite be taken seriously, and since the light touch found in "El Aleph" is lacking, neither can it be considered essentially humorous.

Borges' preoccupation with the thought that a single word or object could be the key to the entire universe—the "emblem" or the "open-sesame"—which might reveal a hidden order or secret plan of the cosmos, is central to much of his work. His interest in numerology, the Kabala, Gnosticism, and the like attest this fact. The compositions just discussed are based upon this notion, as are a number of other prose pieces. Two of these, "La biblioteca de Babel" and "La lotería en Babilonia" will serve to round out our view of this basic Borgesian theme.

"The universe (which others call the Library) is composed of an indefinite and perhaps infinite number of hexagonal galleries . . ." ("El universo [que otros llaman la Biblioteca] se compone de un número indefinido, y tal vez infinito, de galerías hexagonales . . .").[46] Borges tells us in the opening lines of "La biblioteca de Babel." The parenthesis immediately informs us that the particular symbol or emblem of reality to be employed in the piece is the Book, or to be more accurate a collection of books, the Library. Underlying the entire story is the obvious though profound fact that words are symbols and that there is a greater reality behind them. This in turn suggests the parallel notion of philosophical dualism: that the world as we know it is a mere copy of a more real reality. To appreciate the "Biblioteca de Babel" fully, this underlying symbolism must be kept constantly in mind.

The various ways in which the narrator attempts to render the physical aspect of the Library echoes a number of other Borgesian pieces: its form is geometric, an indefinite number of hexagonal galleries placed one atop the other with a central shaft or air space throughout, but its extent is infinite. Like a great circular book, "The Library is a sphere whose exact center is any one of its hexagons and whose circumference is inaccessible" ("La Biblioteca es una esfera cuyo centro cabal es cualquier hexágono, cuya circunferencia es inaccesible").[47] After describing the physical arrangement of the Library, the narrator tells how as a youth he, like all men of the Library, roamed its vast galleries in search of a book, perhaps *the* book, the "catalogue of catalogues." But as he writes he knows death is near and he seems resigned to the fact that he will never know the Library's ultimate secrets. He plans to die near the hexagon in which he was born at which time "there will be no lack of pious hands" ("no faltarán manos piadosas") which will cast his body over the gallery railing into the edifices's vast central air-shaft where it will "sink endlessly and decay and dissolve in the wind generated by the fall, which is infinite" ("se hundirá largamente y se corromperá y disolverá en el viento engendrado por la caída, que es infinita").[48]

There is a definite tone of seriousness—a kind of somber grandeur—which pervades these pages. Unlike "El Aleph" or "El Zahir" there is no blending of mundane reality with the geometrical world of the Library; and what humor appears in the piece, is of a reserved and highly intellectual sort. Borges also shows restraint in the fact that his usual footnotes, bibliographic references, and similar erudite trappings are almost entirely omitted. There are subtle literary echoes and even a few sly references to some of Borges' other works, but the abundance of bookish minutiae which is so evident in his essayistic fiction is absent.

In the main portion of the piece Borges—that is, the nameless narrator—explains the principal "axioms" upon which the Library is organized. First of all, the Library exists eternally; and secondly, there are twenty-five orthographical symbols upon which all of the Library's books are based (twenty-two letters, comma, period, and space). The narrator explains that each book consists of 410 pages; each page, of forty lines; and each line of approximately eighty letters. In brief, the Library is the product of all the possible permutations and combinations of the twenty-five symbols arranged within the format just described. While the number of different volumes would necessarily be incredibly huge, given these specific limitations, it would not be infinite. Yet, the structure of the Library itself, as we just saw, is described in terms clearly suggesting infinitude. Borges' final resolution of the problem posed by the situation—a finite number of items filling an infinite space—is perfectly logical: *"The Library is unlimited and cyclical.* If an eternal traveler were to cross it in any direction,

114   JORGE LUIS BORGES

after centuries he would see that the same volumes were repeated
in the same disorder (which, thus repeated, would be an order:
the Order)" ("Si un eterno viajero la atravesara en cualquier dir-
rección, comprobaría al cabo de los siglos que los mismos vol-
úmenes se repiten en el mismo desorden [que, repetido, sería un
orden: el Orden]").⁴⁹ If we recall that the Library is equated with
the universe, we can see a number of typically Borgesian ideas reflected in this symbolism: if the "books" are thought of as people
or events, notions of cyclical historicism and the idea that there is
nothing really new under the sun immediately come to mind.

But "La biblioteca de Babel" is more than an intellectual exercise in permutation and combination. The "Men of the Library,"
mysterious and tragic figures who roam the endless galleries in
search of general truth or specific answers to troublesome questions, are seldom rewarded for their labors. More often than not
they find only hopelessly garbled volumes which often contain
only one line of tantalizingly clear language. All possible languages—and combinations of language—are found in the *almost*
infinite number of volumes. For example, one "chief of an upper
hexagon" discovers, after much study, that a certain volume is
written in "a Samoyedic Lithuanian dialect of Guarani, with classical Arabian inflections" ("un dialecto samoyedo-lituano del
guaraní, con inflexiones de árabe clásico").⁵⁰ There are virtually
no conceivable orthographic combinations not found in the Library. The narrator tells how, in his own hexagon, may be found
such intriguing titles as *The Combed Thunderclap* (*Trueno pei-
nado*),*The Plaster Cramp* (*El calambre de yeso*), or, even better,
the Tlönian-sounding *Axaxaxas mlö*.⁵¹ Borges notes that "these
phrases at first glance incoherent, can no doubt be justified in a
cryptographical or allegorical manner . . ." ("Esas proposiciones,
a primera vista incoherentes, sin duda son capaces de una
justificación criptográfica o alegórica . . .").⁵² Even more dizzying
is the thought that somewhere in the Library the *key* to such cryptic works must exist! Some of the lonely librarians (their number,
we are told, seems to be steadily diminishing) search for books of
prophecy; others for "vindications," that is, books which "justify"
the existence of a particular individual; while still others seek
among endless galleries of "false" catalogues the "catalogue of
catalogues."

Lurking just below the surface of all this description is a rich and provocative Borgesian allegory of universal history, of man's search for truth, of his ephemeral moments of triumph, of the folly of his sectarian conflicts, and most of all, of the futility of his attempts to solve riddles of an eternal or absolute nature. Borges' description of the "official searchers" as they return from their labors brings out this mood very effectively: "they always arrive extremely tired from their journeys; they speak of a broken stairway which almost killed them . . . sometimes they pick up the nearest volume and leaf through it, looking for infamous words. Obviously, no one expects to discover anything" ("llegan siempre rendidos; hablan de una escalera sin peldaños qué casi los mató; alguna vez, toman el libro más cercano y lo hojean, en busca de palabras infames. Visiblemente, nadie espera descubrir nada").[53] While the "Biblioteca de Babel" has no plotted story, the dramatic allegorical rendering of man's quest sets it apart from Borges' essays and his essayistic fiction. Yet it would be stretching a point to call it a genuine short story; it is, perhaps, one of the finest examples of the uniquely Borgesian *ficción.*

"La lotería en Babilonia" bears some resemblance to the tale just discussed. The term "Babylon" like the word "library" is an emblem or rubric which stands for the universe. In this story, however, Borges emphasizes a slightly different aspect of man's puny efforts to make sense out of an essentially unfathomable world. The broad metaphor of "the lottery" as Borges develops it, deals with the notion that there is a clearly distinguishable difference between "chance happenings" and ordered events. People quite naturally believe—at least before they read "La lotería en Babilonia"—that this is so. After all, theologies have been constructed about the crucial concepts of free will versus determinism, and philosophical systems have used the notions of contingency and necessity as basic building blocks. The nameless narrator of "La lotería," however, comes from a place where these important distinctions are blurred, a "dizzy land where the lottery is the basis of reality" ("un país vertiginoso donde la lotería es parte principal de la realidad").[54]

The story of how the lottery developed from an elementary pastime to become the dominant feature of this world provides the basic material for this piece. The narrator explains how at first the lower classes of Babylon would buy "chances" for a few pennies in the hopes of winning a small prize: barbers were the traditional lottery venders, and drawings were uncomplicated affairs held in the open. Gradually, to encourage interest, a new element was added. Some of those who held "unlucky" numbers not only lost their original investment but also had to pay small fines. If these unfortunate players refused to pay these trifling amounts, the "Company" (for the lottery was now institutionalized and controlled by a mysterious organization) might sue them and even put them in jail. After a while, the losers were not fined at all, but simply incarcerated for a fixed number of days. In this manner the lottery's original monetary basis was altered so that soon winners and losers received both their prizes or punishments in nonmonetary form. A winner might be rewarded by getting an honorific appointment, by having the pleasure of seeing an enemy imprisoned, or by finding "in the peaceful darkness of his room, the woman who begins to excite him and whom he never expected to see again" ("en la pacífica tiniebla del cuarto, la mujer que empieza a inquietarnos o que no esperábamos rever").[55] Losers, as one might imagine, face not only imprisonment but all sorts of infamies including mutilation and death. By this time the "Company" had succeeded in making the operation of the lottery secret, free, and obligatory for all. Further refinements were soon added: a loser's ultimate fate might be altered by a "bifurcation" or lottery-within-the-lottery. The moment before his execution he might be forced to draw nine numbers, one of which could mitigate this extreme penalty, another of which might grant him a full pardon, while yet another might entitle him to a great prize. In like manner, a winner might find a treasure snatched from his grasp at the last moment: "In reality the *number of drawings is infinite*. No decision is final, all branch into others" ("En la realidad *el número de sorteos es infinito*. Ninguna decisión es final, todas se ramifican en otras").[56]

In characteristic Borgesian fashion, the central idea of the all-pervading lottery is unrelentingly carried to its logical conclusion. "Babylon" becomes so thoroughly infused with chance that the very meaning of the word is lost. There are even "impersonal drawings" in which all sorts of improbable actions involving animals or objects are dutifully carried out: "The buyer of a dozen amphoras of Damascene wine will not be surprised if one of them contains a talisman or snake. The scribe who writes a contract almost never fails to introduce some erroneous information . . ."

("El comprador de una docena de ánforas de vino damasceno no se maravillará si una de ellas encierra un talismán o una víbora; el escribano que redacta un contrato no deja casi nunca de introducir algún dato erróneo . . .).[57] Behind all these "chance" happenings is the enigmatic "Company" whose orders, incidentally, *may* not be genuine, but rather the work of "impostors." In such a world who can distinguish what is counterfeit from what is genuine? In the last paragraph of the piece the narrator concludes, "The Company's silent operations, comparable to God's, gives rise to all sorts of conjectures . . . that the Company has not existed for centuries and that the sacred disorder of our lives is purely hereditary, traditional . . . that the Company is omnipotent, but that it only has influence in tiny things. . . . Another, in the words of masked heresiarchs, *that it has never existed and will not exist.* Another, no less vile, reasons that it is indifferent to affirm or deny the reality of the shadowy corporation, because Babylon is nothing else than an infinite game of chance" ("Ese funcionamiento silencioso, comparable al de Dios, provoca toda suerte de conjeturas . . . que hace ya siglos que no existe la Compañía y que el sacro desorden de nuestras vidas es puramente hereditario, tradicional . . . que la Compañía es omnipotente, pero que sólo influye en cosas minúsculas. Otra, por boca de heresiarcas enmascarados, que no ha existido nunca y no existirá. Otra, no menos vil, razona que es indiferente afirmar o negar la realidad de la tenebrosa corporación, porque Babilonia no es otra cosa que un infinito juego de azares).[58]

Like "La biblioteca . . ." the impact of "La lotería . . ." derives from Borges' relentless and vertiginous expansion of a relatively simple idea into nightmarish proportions. Both pieces, richly allegorical yield a picture of man's futile attempts to set up intellectual constructs which might help him comprehend the universe. Unsuccessful as these attempts may be, Borges' description of the very human quality of striving gives these pages a dramatic tension which is not nearly as evident in his essayistic fiction.

III *Short Stories*

Borges' critics have often noted that real characters—believable flesh-and-blood people—are almost entirely absent in his work. Borges himself has repeatedly stated that the creation of fully developed, psychologically convincing literary personalities has never been one of his objectives. In his essays we saw how he even doubted that *any* writer can attain this objective. To this point in the examination of his prose fiction we have met few if any "real" people in the sense demanded by Borges' critics. In several of the pieces, moreover, the central personality has been merely a nameless narrator or the author himself. By contrast, in those compositions which conform more to the structure of the traditional short story Borges places greater emphasis on developing his plots around a central figure. These figures, whether they be the renegade John Vincent Moon, the enigmatic "Gray Man" of the "Ruinas circulares," the detective Erik Lönnrot, or the autobiographic Dahlman, have considerably more substance than a Pierre Menard or an Ireneo Funes. Yet Borges neither wishes to write character studies nor stories which pretend to render a complete and accurate picture of society. To judge him by these standards makes little sense. In the pieces just discussed, his characters are subordinated to an idea or philosophic concept which he wishes to illustrate. In the pieces to follow, they tend to be a function of plot, of narrative for narrative's sake, though Borges never forsakes his favorite philosophical notions.

The mystical idea that all men are one, and its corollary that under certain circumstances the villain may be a hero, or vice versa, has appeared frequently in Borges' work. Even his interest in the Gnostic inversion of good and evil—the Judas figure, for example—may be related to his conviction that only the finest of lines divides the world's saints and heroes from its most despised villains. Several stories revolve about this theme, notably "La forma de la espada" ("The Shape of the Sword") and the "Tema del héroe y el traidor" ("Theme of the Hero and the Traitor"). Borges' fascination with the notion of ambivalence in personality may well be a reflection of his own psyche. Though the temptation to psychoanalyze is great, it should be resisted: suffice it to say that despite his retiring manner, Borges has always been intrigued by bandits, *compadritos* and by men of action and violence. But aside from the theme's psychological or philosophical ramifications, it certainly provides the basis for a good story.

"El tema del traidor y el héroe" Borges tells us, might have taken place in any "oppressed and tenacious country." The scene of action, however, is Ireland; the year, about 1824. The narrator,

Ryan, is our contemporary, but his tale concerns Fergus Kilpatrick, his great-grandfather. Kilpatrick was a celebrated hero of the early Irish independence movement who died at the hands of an unknown assassin. Certain circumstances surrounding his death, Ryan discovers, were rather unusual. For one thing, he was shot in a theater while watching *Macbeth,* whose tragedy, Borges notes, "prefigured" that of Kilpatrick. Another curious detail is inserted with the remark that the hero's grave was mysteriously violated. Ryan, through considerable historical detective work, pieces together the true story of his ancestor's death. It seems that at the last rebel meeting over which he presided, Kilpatrick signed a death order for the execution of a traitor, yet strangely, the name of the culprit was deleted from this document. Ryan finally deciphers the mystery of this omission: Kilpatrick, having been discovered as a traitor, agreed to sign his own death warrant. Since he knew that his fellow conspirators would execute him anyway, and since all Ireland worshiped him as a hero and the shining hope of the movement, he remained enough of a patriot to cooperate in a scheme which offered him the possibility of redeeming himself. Presumably his original act of treason was motivated more by material gain than by the desire to sabotage the Irish independence movement. And so Kilpatrick was shot "in deliberately dramatic circumstances." In this way he became a martyr, and even in death, served the Irish cause.

Ryan's discovery of his great-grandfather's true colors is revealed about halfway through his sketchy piece. Borges makes no attempt to keep the reader in suspense; rather, he seems more concerned with pointing out a number of parallelisms between Kilpatrick's death and that of Julius Caesar, Shakespeare's *Macbeth,* and even Abraham Lincoln. The basic narrative is, moreover, placed within a rather heavy "double frame." Borges first introduces Ryan, he then describes Ryan's thoughts as he constructs the events of 1824, and finally he presents, through Ryan, the actual kernel of Kilpatrick's story. The piece is more of a plot outline than a real short story, a fact which Borges himself makes clear at the outset: "in my idle afternoons I have imagined this story plot which I shall perhaps write some day . . ." ("he imaginado este argumento, que escribiré tal vez . . . en las tardes inútiles . . .").[59]

"A spiteful scar crossed his face: an ash-colored and nearly perfect arc that creased his temple at one tip and his cheek at the other. His real name is of no importance . . ." ("Le cruzaba la cara una cicatriz rencorosa: un arco ceniciento y casi perfecto que de un lado ajaba la sien y del otro el pómulo. Su nombre verdadero no importa . . .").[60] With this vigorous description Borges introduces the protagonist of "La forma de la espada." We learn that "the Englishman," as his Latin American neighbors call him, is in fact a hard-drinking, cruel, taciturn Irishman who has immigrated to the border country of southern Brazil and northern Argentina. How he earns his living is uncertain: some say he's a smuggler, others a sugar grower. One evening, a sudden rise in a river forces Borges, who presumably had been traveling in the region, to spend an evening with this colorful expatriate. The two strike up an after-dinner conversation in the course of which "the Englishman" relates his adventures as a rebel in the Irish independence movement.

The central figure in his tale is John Vincent Moon, another young rebel whom he describes as "slender and flaccid at the same time; he gave the impression of being invertebrate" ("Era flaco y fofo a la vez; daba la incómoda impresión de ser invertebrado").[61] As the tale develops, it becomes clear that Moon was, in sharp contrast to the narrator, a coward. Moon flees the thick of battle, makes much of a superficial wound, and is given to nervous sobbing when the going gets rough. The fortunes of the revolution meanwhile take a turn for the worse, and the city which the Irish rebels were trying to hold falls to the British. One afternoon, the narrator discovers Moon talking on the telephone—obviously to the enemy, and obviously informing on the Irish. Infuriated, he pursues the traitor, seizes him, and then, using an old curved cutlass from the wall of the house in which they were staying, carves into Moon's face "a half-moon of blood." As "the Englishman" relates these events his hands begin shaking. When Borges inquires as to the ultimate fate of the traitor, he is told that "He collected his Judas money and fled to Brazil" ("Cobró los dineros de Judas y huyó al Brasil").[62] At this point the narrator cannot continue; when urged to go on, he blurts out the truth "Don't you see that I carry written on my face the mark of my infamy? I have told you the story thus so that you would hear me to the end . . .

I am Vincent Moon. Now despise me" ("¿No ve que llevo escrita en la cara la marca de mi infamia? Le he narrado la historia de este modo para que la oyera hasta el fin . . . yo soy Vincent Moon. Ahora despréciceme").[63]

Both the framing device and the "switch" at the end are old techniques in the art of fiction. Certainly they are familar to readers of detective tales and other popular genres. As in the best examples of this kind of work, there is a certain pleasure in reexamining the story to find the thinly veiled clues which hint at the final outcome. Such clues abound in Borges' tale. The very first line mentions the "*spiteful* scar" on the "Englishman's" face; before the narrator begins his story he tells Borges that he's not English but Irish, at which point he is described as "stopping short, as if he had revealed a secret" ("Dicho esto se detuvo, como si hubiera revelado un secreto");[64] and at the start of his narration, he mentions that many of his comrades were by now dead, including "the most worthy, who died in the courtyard of a barracks" ("el que más valía, murió en el patio de un cuartel").[65] Like the other clues, this last one is obviously a reference to the rebel leader whom Moon denounced to the British; but like all good clues, they only become obvious after the cat is let out of the bag. As the "Englishman" reveals more of his story, the clues become more frequent and perhaps more obvious: the fact that Moon, though young and new to the group, was constantly inquiring into the plans of the rebel unit is a case in point. Near the end of the piece Borges inserts a hint in the form of an essayistic digression which almost ruins the story's final impact. The narrator describing Moon says "This frightened man mortified me, as if I were the coward, not Vincent Moon. Whatever one man does, it is as if all men did it. For that reason it is not unfair that one disobedience in a garden should contaminate all humanity; for that reason it is not unjust that the crucifixion of a single Jew should be sufficient to save it. Perhaps Schopenhauer was right: I am all other men; any man is all men, Shakespeare is in some manner the miserable John Vincent Moon" ("Me abochornaba ese hombre con miedo, como si yo fuera el cobarde, no Vincent Moon. Lo que hace un hombre es como si lo hicieran todos los hombres. Por eso no es injusto que una desobediencia en un jardín contamine al género humano; por eso no es injusto que la crucifixión de un solo judío

baste para salvarlo. Acaso Schopenhauer tiene razón: yo soy los
otros, cualquier hombre es todos los hombres, Shakespeare es de
algún modo el miserable John Vincent Moon").[66]

Though Borges' celebrated tale "Las ruinas circulares" is very
different in theme, its structure parallels that of "La forma de la
espada" in that the denouement depends on the revelation of the
protagonist's identity. And, like the stories just discussed, once his
identity is known, it is possible to re-examine the tale and find
indications of what was to come. The structure of "Las ruinas
circulares" is however, only one of its many attractions. In few, if
any, of his other stories is Borges' prose style more effective. The
language, rhythmic and at times extremely poetic, creates a mood
and texture that compliments the theme of the piece with remarkable fidelity. Though the philosophical content of "Las ruinas circulares" is apparent to anyone familiar with Borges' work, in contrast to some of his stories, it seldom intrudes upon the narrative
flow.

The opening lines of the story reveal these stylistic qualities
particularly well: "No one saw him disembark in the unanimous
night, no one saw the bamboo canoe sinking into the sacred mud,
but within a few days no one was unaware that the silent man
came from the South and that his home was one of the infinite
villages upstream on the violent side of the mountain, where the
Zend tongue is not contaminated with Greek . . ." ("Nadie lo vió
desembarcar en la unánime noche, nadie vió la canoa de bambú
sumiéndose en el fango sagrado, pero a los pocos días nadie
ignoraba que el hombre taciturno venía del Sur y que su patria
era una de las infinitas aldeas que están aguas arriba, en el
flanco violento de la montaña, donde el idioma zend no está
contaminado de griego . . .").[67] The mysterious traveler, described as "the gray man," kisses the mud, ascends the river
bank, without pushing aside the brambles which "dilacerated" his
flesh, and lies exhausted and asleep. A significant detail which
Borges notes in parenthesis is that he "probably did not feel" the
thorns as he passed through them.

The spot where the stranger lies asleep is a "circular enclosure
crowned by a stone horse or tiger, which once was the color of fire
and now was that of ashes. This circle was a temple, long ago
devoured by fire . . ." ("Ese redondel es un templo que devora-
ron los incendios antiguos . . .").[68] Upon awakening, Borges tells

us, the man knows that this is the precise place required to carry out his "purpose," the exact nature of which is clarified shortly: "The purpose which guided him was not impossible, though it was supernatural. He wanted to dream a man: he wanted to dream him with minute integrity and insert him into reality" ("El propósito que lo guiaba no era imposible, aunque sí sobrenatural. Quería soñar un hombre: quería soñarlo con integridad minuciosa e imponerlo a la realidad").[69] What follows is the detailed description of how the protagonist goes about his task.

At first he attempts to dream a "class" of disciples—a large group from whom he might select, or "redeem," a single individual to "insert" into reality. After a number of unsuccessful efforts he decides that he must concentrate intensely on just one of the group. But his attempt fails; he suffers insomnia; he becomes infuriated and frustrated. Finally he comes to the conclusion that he must abandon his original method completely. He spends a month recuperating his powers before again undertaking his arduous task. He gives up *trying* to dream and as a result, he finds he sleeps more easily and that once again he is able to dream. Ready to begin his project anew, "he purified himself in the waters of the river, worshiped the planetary gods, uttered the permitted syllables of a powerful name and slept" ("se purificó en las aguas del río, adoró los dioses planetarios, pronunció las sílabas lícitas de un nombre poderoso y durmió.[70] At this point he dreams of a beating heart. He now understands how he can accomplish his objective. As a sculptor carefully chisels a masterpiece, the "gray man" slowly fashions his creation. Starting with the internal organs he painstakingly dreams the arteries, the skeleton, and the eyelids. "The innumerable hair was perhaps the most difficult task" ("El pelo innumerable fué tal vez la tarea más difícil"),[71] he tells us. After a year, the dream child is physically complete. Finally, "In the dreamer's dream, the dreamed one awoke" ("En el sueño del hombre que soñaba, el soñado se despertó").[72]

The protagonist devotes some two years to instructing his child in the mysteries of the universe and in the enigmatic details of the "fire cult." The son is now ready to leave: his father kisses him and sends him off to another temple far downstream where, presumably, he would fulfill his duties as a priest of his cult. However, before he departs, his father instills in him the "complete oblivion of his years of apprenticeship" ("el olvido total de sus años de

aprendizaje").[73] His purpose in doing this, as Borges notes parenthetically, is to make him think that he is a man, not a phantom.
At any rate, the son leaves, and the parent, saddened by his departure, is left to meditate. His thoughts continue to be troubled
by the fear that his son might in some way learn that his existence
was merely illusory, and, he muses, "Not to be a man, to be the
projection of another man's dream, what a feeling of humiliation,
of vertigo!" ("No ser un hombre, ser la proyección del sueño de
otro hombre, ¡qué humillación incomparable, qué, vértigo!").[74]

At this point in the story, smoke appears in the distance; then
the flight of animals: finally the "gray man" realizes that a ring of
fire is closing in on him. At first he thinks of trying to escape into
the river; but he is old and tired, and he knows that inevitable
death is coming to "absolve him of his labors." The flames come
closer and begin to engulf him. But he feels neither heat nor com-
bustion. The last two lines of the tale reveal what the astute
reader has perhaps already guessed: "With relief, with humiliation, with terror, he understood that he too was a mere appearance, dreamt by another" ("Con alivio, con humillación, con terror, comprendió que él también era una apariencia, que otro
estaba soñándolo").[75]

A wealth of Borgesian ideas underlies the story: the Berkeleyan
notion of existence as a function of perception carried to the extreme of "dreaming" objects into the real world, is blended with
Gnostic cosmology and the idea of a creator-behind-the-creator.
The suggestion of an infinite regression also is evident: the "gray
man" dreams a son who quite naturally will dream another son,
and so on. Yet these ideas lie just below the surface. Except for a
brief mention of the Gnostics and the ancient cult of fire, the story
flows smoothly along in the best tradition of genuine fantastic fiction. And, as in detective stories, the most minute details become
significant once we know the story's final outcome: for example,
the color *gray* which Borges first uses to describe his protagonist,
clearly suggests his shadowy existence; the early mention of *another* distant temple may well be a reference to the protagonist's
own origins; and his careful plan to erase all memory of his son's
creation may be viewed as an echo of what had been done to him.
To sum up, the balancing of all these elements—the underlying
philosophic concepts, the mood and language of genuine fantasy,

and the structure of a detective story—have produced one of Borges' most impressive compositions.

Borges' obvious fascination with detective fiction comes to the fore in several of his better-known stories. One such tale, "La muerte y la brújula" ("Death and the Compass") is in fact a legitimate example of the genre, considerably modified, though it retains a distinctively Borgesian flavor. For one thing, the solution of the series of crimes presented in the story is achieved through the protagonist's application of a bit of Kabalistic hocus-pocus: for another, the tale is infused with considerable—though underplayed—humor. The plot of "La muerte y la brújula" is not especially unusual; reduced to essentials, it involves three murders which occur at intervals of exactly one month apart and at locations which, when traced on a map, form an equilateral triangle. The super-sleuth Erik Lönnrot, like a number of Borges' protagonists, is clever but not quite clever enough. He concludes that a fourth murder is to occur and that its time and place would be defined by forming a diamond-shaped figure on the base of the equilateral triangle. He traces the point on a map of the city and goes there exactly one month after the third murder. The exact spot happens to be a labyrinthine country estate full of Borgesian detail: "the villa . . . abounded in pointless symmetries and in maniacal repetitions" ("la casa de la quinta . . . abundaba en inútiles simetrías y en repeticiones maniáticas").[76] Lönnrot, hoping to forestall the crime and capture the killer, reaches the precise point indicated by his calculations, whereupon he is seized by two men, is disarmed, is informed in excruciating detail of how he has been lured to the spot, and is of course killed by his enemy and arch-criminal, Red Scharlach, alias "The Dandy."

Unless the reader of "La muerte y la brújula" is especially fond of detective stories as such, the charm of the piece resides in its fundamental irony, the interplay of Borgesian ideas, and in the tale's frequent sly bits of humor. The scene of the story is itself delightfully unlikely: a Talmudic congress at an unnamed French city which is, as Borges' commentators have pointed out, nothing more than a thinly veiled double of Buenos Aires. The characters in the tale are an equally unlikely group: the first victim, the scholarly rabbi of Podolsk, and student of Kabala, Dr. Marcel Yarmolinsky; the protagonist, the super-sleuth Erik Lönnrot, a man of "reckless discernment"; Red Scharlach, author of the

"fiendish series" of killings; the enigmatic third victim, one Ginsburg, also known as "Gryphius"; the innkeeper, Black Finnegan;
various thugs, harlequins (the period covered by the crimes includes Carnival); and a "myopic, shy atheist" who is the editor of
the *Yidische Zaitung.* The two principal characters have names
which tempt the reader into blind alleys of deduction: why, for
example, should the detective's name be Lönnrot (i.e., Lönn-*red*)
and the criminal's name be *Red Scharlach* (Sharlach = Scarlet)?

The device by which Lönnrot is duped could not be more Borgesian. The four points which indicate the four "murders" (actually only three, since we learn at the tale's end that the third was a
hoax) correspond to the mystic figure of the tetragrammaton, a
Kabalistic emblem of the four Hebrew letters, JHVH, which make
up the name of God. Sharlach, who was an old enemy of Lönnrot
and who had sworn to kill him (this ridiculously obvious hint is
given in the tale's first paragraph!), carefully designed the crimes
knowing full well that his enemy would follow all the deliberately
placed clues and thus fall into his trap. With infinite *sang froid,*
Scharlach tells his victim, just before he shoots him, the details of
the complex plan: "I . . . interspersed repeated signs that would
allow you, Erik Lönnrot, the reasoner, to understand that the
series was quadruple. A portent in the north, others in the east
and west, demand a fourth portent in the south. . . . I sent the
equilateral triangle to (Inspector) Treviranus. I foresaw that you
would add the missing point . . . the point which fixes in ad-
vance where a punctual death awaits you. I have premeditated
everything . . ." ("Yo . . . intercalé repetidos indicios para
que usted, el razonador Erik Lönnrot, comprendiera que es cuádruple. Un prodigio en el Norte, otros en el Este y en el Oeste,
reclaman un cuarto prodigio en el Sur. . . . Yo mandé el trián-
gulo equilátero a Treviranus. Yo presentí que usted agregaría el
punto que falta . . . el punto que prefija el lugar donde una ex-
acta muerte lo espera. Todo lo he premeditado . . .")[77]

The ironies that underlie the "La muerte y la brújula" should be
obvious to those who knew Borges well. Note that Sharlach ad-
dresses Lönnrot as "you, the reasoner." The detective is just that.
Like most men who have faith in reason, he attempts to find some
scheme, some plan to his little universe; but in trying to be clever
he finds only defeat and death. As in "La biblioteca de Babel," as
in "Las ruinas circulares," or as in any number of other pieces,

Borges is again underscoring the theme of human vanity and futility. Perhaps the ultimate irony of "La muerte y la brújula" lies in the fact that the very first "crime" was merely a mistake—Yarmolinsky was killed by a drunken thug who was supposed to be robbing the room across the hall. In this manner a *chance* happening provides the opportunity for Scharlach to build his entire plot. Thus, even in the designs of the gods—for Sharlach, in his almost omnipotent manipulation of the situation seems to have godlike powers—chance may well play an important role.

The revelation of the protagonist's—or the antagonist's—identity is, as we have seen, one of Borges' favorite devices. In most of the stories which depend upon highly developed plots, some variation of this technique appears. In the piece just discussed, Red Sharlach remains on the sidelines—even to the point of criticizing the police for not solving the series of murders—until at the very end he is revealed as the mastermind behind the crimes; in "La forma de la espada," Moon's true identity is the central fact of the denouement; and in "Las ruinas circulares" the protagonist's final realization of who he is, or what he is, provides the magnificent climax to this widely acclaimed tale. An unusual variation of this device forms the superstructure of another of Borges' better-known stories, "El jardín de senderos que se bifurcan."

On the surface, "El jardín . . ." may be thought of as a spy story—a genre certainly akin to detective fiction. The narrative is related in the form of a dictated statement of a Dr. Yu Tsun whom we learn, as the tale unfolds, is in England and is awaiting execution as a condemned agent for the Germans during World War I. The plot, leaving out considerable rich internal detail, is quite simple. Yu Tsun is a Chinese professor of English who had taught at a German school in Tsing Tao. For motives which are not entirely clear, though pride in his race seems to be one, he becomes an agent for the Germans. His specific objective in this story is to communicate to Berlin the exact name of the town in which the British were massing their artillery preparatory to a major offensive. However, the protagonist's immediate superior, one Viktor Runeberg,[78] has been captured, and hence Yu knows that his normal lines of communication to Berlin no longer exist, that the British agents are surely aware of his own identity as a spy, and that even now they are hot on his trail. Convinced that escape is impossible, he nonetheless is determined to communicate his information to Berlin. In the space of ten minutes he devises a plan, the nature of which is only revealed at the story's end. He studies the telephone directory in his room and enigmatically observes that it "listed the name of the only person capable of transmitting the message; he lived in the suburb of Fenton, less than a half hour's ride away" ("me dió el nombre de la única persona capaz de transmitir la noticia: vivía en un suburbio de Fenton, a menos de media hora de tren").[79] Yu quickly takes the train for the suburb, and even as it leaves the station he sees the British agent Madden running desperately down the platform after him. Arriving in the country, he hurries to the home of a Mr. Stephen Albert, who, by a strange coincidence, happens to be a former missionary to China and an ardent sinologist. Albert, who apparently mistakes his visitor for an acquaintance in the Chinese consular service, invites Yu in. The two soon become engaged in a discussion of the work of one Ts'ui Pên, an ancient Chinese astrologer and writer who was, coincidentally, an ancestor of the protagonist. Since Yu calculates that it will be an hour before his pursuers can overtake him, he chats amiably with Albert about the ancient sage and the literary labyrinth which he had composed—an unusual book, entitled *The Garden of the Forking Paths* (*El jardín de senderos que se bifurcan*). But Yu's brief hour hurries by, and finally he is forced to perform the act which had brought him to this particular place. When his hosts' back is turned, Yu Tsun carefully withdraws his revolver and kills Stephen Albert. At this moment the British agent Madden breaks in and arrests Yu. In the last paragraph of the story we learn that the newspaper reports of the murder of one Stephen Albert by a certain Yu Tsun reach Berlin, and that from them the chief German intelligence officer easily extracts a vital bit of information: namely, that the British were massing artillery, preparatory for an offensive at the Belgian town of Albert. At the tale's conclusion Yu Tsun explains: "The chief had deciphered this mystery. He knew my problem was to indicate (through the uproar of the war) the city called Albert, and that I had found no other means to do so than to kill a man of that name. He does not know (no one can know) my innumerable contrition and weariness" ("El Jefe ha discifrado ese enigma. Sabe que mi problema era indicar [a través del estrépito de la guerra] la ciudad que se llama Albert y que no hallé otro medio que matar a una persona de ese nombre. No sabe [nadie puede saber] mi innumerable contrición y cansancio").[80]

"El jardín de senderos que se bifurcan," though one of Borges' most popular stories, suffers from several important defects. For one thing, given the rather implausible, and certainly artificial nature of the plot, Borges seems too serious. The lightness and humor of "La muerte y la brújula" or "El Aleph" are conspicuous by their absence. For another, the long discussion of the ancient Chinese labyrinth appears to be little more than a reworking of material Borges has expressed better elsewhere. Some of the ideas —those dealing with time, for example—may strike the readers of science fiction and fantasy as rather commonplace. Albert's explanation of Ts'ui Pên's concept of time exemplifies the point: "In contrast to Newton and Schopenhauer, your ancestor did not believe in a uniform, absolute time. He believed in an infinite series of times, in a growing, dizzying net of divergent, convergent and parallel times" ("A diferencia de Newton y de Schopenhauer, su antepasado no creía en un tiempo uniforme, absoluto. Creía en infinitas series de tiempos, en una red creciente y vertiginosa de tiempos divergentes, convergentes y paralelos").[81] On several occasions during the course of this erudite conversation on time, ancient China, and novelistic bifurcations, the protagonist recalls that he felt a mysterious "swarming sensation" ("una . . . intangible pululación") and that his host's English garden seemed to be peopled by invisible beings. Borges obviously is trying to create the feeling that another plane of existence—perhaps some distant time period—was in some manner impinging on our world. In short, this tale presents one of the very few cases of Borges' attempting to insert a genuine element of fantasy into an essentially realistic, if unlikely, narrative. In other pieces where he has attempted to do this, in "Tlön" or in "El Aleph" for example, the perils of mixing the real and the fantastic are greatly mitigated by a generous dose of Borgesian humor. And since this all-important element is not present in "El jardín de senderos que se bifurcan" the story seems, at least to the writer, unconvincing. In this respect, it recalls "El Zahir," which, it was noted, suffers from similar defects.

"El inmortal" is a very different kind of tale, but one in which the revelation of the protagonist's identity is handled in an intellectually more stimulating manner. Although "El inmortal" is clearly a story, the underlying ideas rather than a superimposed plot determine its structure. And unlike the tale just examined, the fantastic elements are so completely unreal that we accept them as we do myths, with little hesitation. The piece begins with Francis Bacon's scriptural quotation, "Solomon saith, *There is no new thing upon the earth. . . .*" Borges then describes a manuscript, written in English but abounding in Latinisms, found in an old edition of Pope's *Iliad*. The story which follows, we are told, is a literal rendition of this old document. At the tale's end Borges adds a "postscript" in which he discusses several scholarly opinions of the mysterious manuscript. This "postscript," together with a related footnote, are examples of Borges' chronic literary gamesmanship: though they may serve to complete the framing device established in the introduction, they seem to be unnecessary adjuncts to a story quite capable of standing on its own feet.

The tale is told in the first person. The narrator is apparently a Roman officer of the time of the Emperor Diocletian. One morning, at dawn, an "exhausted and bloody horseman" arrives at his camp: his last words describe a certain "river of immortality" which he was seeking. The narrator resolves to find this river and the City of the Immortals which lies on its banks. The protagonist-narrator, whose name we soon learn is Marcus Flaminus Rufus, then describes his wanderings in quest of the city and river. Borges' prose on these pages is some of his finest: at times it possesses a rhythmic grandeur suggestive of epic literature, at other times, it recalls the best of fantasy or science fiction. The protagonist's discovery of the City of Immortals (which seems to exist somewhere in Asia Minor) reads almost like the description of a landing on an alien planet. The city is inhabited by troglodytes, "naked, gray-skinned, scraggly bearded men" ("hombres de piel gris, de barba negligente, desnudos")[82], who can barely speak and who eat serpents. The city itself, in contrast to the primitive or degenerate aspect of this race of men, has a magnificent, complex, and "obfuscating" grandeur. The narrator describes in considerable detail the maze of walls, chambers, multiple doorways, and passages which make the outer fringes of the city a true labyrinth. Once in the "resplendent" city he discovers to his horror that its central palace is in fact a labyrinth within a labyrinth: "It abounded in dead-end corridors, high unattainable windows, portentous doors which led to a cell or pit, incredible inverted stairways whose steps and balustrades hung downwards . . ."

("Abundaban el corredor sin salida, la alta ventana inalcanzable, la aparatosa puerta que daba a una celda o a un pozo, las increíbles escaleras inversas, con los peldaños y la balaustrada hacia abajo").[83]

Finally, he extricates himself from the nightmarish palace and city, but waiting for him just outside is one of the troglodytes who had earlier followed him to that point, much as would a faithful hound. The creature reminds him of Argos, Ulysses' "moribund old dog," and so, he begins to call him "Argos." Finally, after a portentous night of torrential rain, the troglodyte miraculously manages to speak. He stammers out the few words, "Argos, Ulysses' dog." At this point the stunned narrator comments: "We accept reality easily, perhaps because we intuit that nothing is real. I asked him what he knew of the *Odyssey*. The exercise of Greek was painful for him; I had to repeat the question. *'Very little,'* he said. *'Less than the poorest rhapsodist. It must be a thousand and one hundred years since I invented it'*" ("Fácilmente aceptamos la realidad, acaso porque intuimos que nada es real. Le pregunté qué sabía de la Odisea. La práctica del griego le era penosa; tuve que repetir la pregunta. *Muy poco*, dijo. *Menos que el rapsoda más pobre. Ya habrán pasado mil cien años desde que la inventé*").[84]

After this initial revelation, everything about the City of the Immortals and its inhabitants becomes clear: the troglodytes were the Immortals; their original great city had been razed some nine centuries before: and in its place they built the "mad" city, "A kind of parody or inversion and also temple of the irrational gods who govern the world" ("Suerte de parodia o reverso y también templo de los dioses irracionales que manejan el mundo").[85] Since they had come to the conclusion that all undertakings were in vain, after erecting the labyrinthine city the Immortals decided to pursue the life of pure speculation, doing absolutely nothing and living in caves outside the city. These facts, and many others are related by the troglodyte who is, in effect, the Homer of ancient Greece.

The next few pages of the story are deliberately hazy. The narrator philosophizes on immortality and on the theme that "one single immortal man is all men" ("un solo hombre inmortal es todos los hombres").[86] He begins to use the plural pronoun "we" in place of the first-person singular. He refers to works of literature

—the twelfth-century *Poem of the Cid*, for example—which were as yet unwritten in the time of Diocletian. In short, the span of a normal lifetime is forgotten, and the mysterious narrator has apparently become one of the Immortals. He tells us that he parted company with Homer at the gates of Tangier; he then traveled far and wide, fighting with Harold at Hastings in 1066; later "in the Seventh Century of the Hegira" he transcribed the tales of Sinbad; still later, in seventeenth-century Europe, he studied astrology; in 1714 he was in Aberdeen with Pope when the latter did his *Iliad;* a few years later, he discussed the origins of this same epic with one Giambattista (Vico, presumably); and so on into the twentieth century. A small but significant detail crops up toward the end of this lengthy narrative. One day in 1921, the protagonist drinks from a clear spring just outside an ancient city on the coast of Eritrea. He then accidently pricks his hand on a thorn and discovers to his joy and incredulity, that a drop of blood forms: once again he is mortal. He re-examines the narrative just presented and discovers in it (as do the readers of Borges' tale) certain inconsistencies. He then explains: "The story I have narrated seems unreal because in it are mixed the events of two different men" ("La historia que he narrado parece irreal porque en ella se mezclan los sucesos de dos hombres distintos").[87] The person of Flaminus Rufus, the Roman soldier blends and flows into the figure of Homer. Rufus could lose his identity as an individual because he drank of the river of immortality; and, as "the narrator" pointed out earlier, "one single immortal man is all men." His compound identity now revealed, the once immortal protagonist solemnly declares: "I have been Homer; shortly, I shall be No One, like Ulysses; shortly, I shall be all men; I shall be dead" ("Yo he sido Homero; en breve, seré Nadie, como Ulises; en breve, seré todos: estaré muerto").[88]

"El inmortal" is one of Borges' most ambitious stories. In it he tries—and with considerable success—to combine the sparkling intellectuality of his best philosophic essays, the far-ranging erudition of his literary studies, and the highly imaginative prose of his best *ficciones*. Some may feel that he has attempted to do too much within the limits of the piece's original twenty pages. It is certainly not one of Borges' most easily digested compositions; yet for the devoted Borges *aficionado*, "El inmortal" may be one of his most impressive creations.

It would be both impractical and tedious to attempt a detailed analysis of all of Borges' stories. The pieces discussed have provided an adequate general view of themes and structural devices representative of his prose fiction. But before concluding there remain several important tales which merit at least passing notice. Some of these, "Emma Zunz" or "El milagro secreto," for example, may be atypical; but for this reason alone, one should be aware of them. Others, such as "El fin" or "Biografía de Tadeo Isidoro Cruz" may mean little to foreign readers but serve to demonstrate the fact that Borges' roots—despite his cosmopolitanism—go deep into the rich Argentine soil.

Critics of Borges have often commented on the remarkable absence of women in his fiction. This omission is all the more inexplicable when we recall that some of his finest poetry was inspired by women, was dedicated to women, or was, quite simply, love poetry. In only one of his stories, "Emma Zunz," does a female protagonist appear. Even as minor characters women are seldom found in his fiction, though they do have some importance in a few tales such as "El hombre de la esquina rosada" or the "Historia del guerrero y la cautiva" ("History of the Warrior and the Captive"). It is of some significance that the plot for "Emma Zunz" was not Borges' own, but was suggested to him by a friend, Cecilia Ingenieros. Be that as it may, "Emma Zunz" is the story of a young girl's scheme to avenge the ruination and death of her father. Accused of embezzling from his employer, Mr. Zunz flees his country and eventually commits suicide. Before fleeing, however, he revealed to his daughter the fact that the company manager—one Aaron Lowenthal—was the real thief. Years later, when Emma learns of her father's solitary death she devises a bizarre plan to ruin Lowenthal, now riding high as one of the company's owners. She arranges a meeting with her intended victim, but before arriving she visits the waterfront district, affecting the appearance of a prostitute. A nondescript Scandinavian sailor picks her up, takes her to a squalid room, deflowers her, and quickly leaves. Emma, as soon as this loathsome interlude is concluded, hurries to Lowenthal's home and shoots him. She then picks up the phone and reports "Something incredible has happened. . . . Mr. Lowenthal had me come over on a pretext. . . . He abused me. I killed him . . ." ("Ha ocurrido una cosa que es increíble. . . . El señor Loewenthal me hizo venir con el

pretexto . . . Abusó de mí, lo maté . . .").[89] Borges ends the
tale by noting that everyone seemed convinced of the veracity of
Emma's story; one gathers that her plan was a complete success.
But for a few revealing details, if "Emma Zunz" were anony-
mously listed in a collection of stories, most readers would probably not guess the identity of its author. In short, though it is not a
bad piece of fiction, "Emma Zunz" is one of the least "Borgesian"
of the tales we have examined.

Any survey of Borges' fiction would be incomplete without considering a few pieces whose thematic material is drawn from native Argentine sources. The foreign reader, unless he happens to
be familiar with certain Argentine traditions and with specific literary works, may have difficulty in appreciating these stories to
the fullest extent. When Borges writes his fictional footnotes to
Homer, to Coleridge, to Cervantes or to Shakespeare he can be
certain of having a wide and discerning audience. However, when
he takes José Hernández' nineteenth-century gauchesque poem
Martín Fierro as his point of departure, his audience will be necessarily limited.

The structure of "Biografía de Tadeo Isidoro Cruz," a story
which illustrates this problem perfectly, is quite simple. Borges
sketches the early life of the protagonist as if he were a historical
figure. He gives his exact birth date, his years of service in the
army, and so on. Borges notes several gaps in this biography, but
he underscores important events, such as Cruz' being made a sergeant in the rural police in the year 1869. The tale ends with a
dramatic incident one day in June of the following year. Cruz is
ordered to capture a dangerous gaucho outlaw, the known killer
of two men. In attempting to carry out this mission, he is impressed by the valor of his opponent: he realizes that his destiny is
to join him, rather than to fight him. He dimly comprehends that
the gauchesque values which this so-called criminal represents
are values which he himself cherishes, and so he deserts his men
and becomes the steadfast companion of the pursued gaucho,
Martín Fierro. Though Borges withholds the identity of Cruz's
opponent until the last line, those familiar with Hernández' poem
realize what is happening well before the end. In the original
Martín Fierro, of course, nothing is revealed about Cruz's background until after he joins forces with Fierro. Borges has in effect
developed a parallel story line which "intersects" with the narra-

tive of Hernández' poem at the point where Seargent Cruz first appears.

A variant of this device is employed in "El fin." In this tale the brother of one of Fierro's victims, "The Negro," challenges Fierro to a duel and subsequently kills him. The background for the story—Fierro's knifing of the original "Negro"—is part of the *Martín Fierro*, but the brother's vengeance is purely Borges' invention. Much of the dramatic impact results from the fact that the death of Fierro, as depicted by Borges, is an exact replica of the original killing; except for the fact that the roles of victim and killer are reversed. Yet the Borges blending of apparently opposed identities can hardly be appreciated without some knowledge of the tale's literary background.

Borges has written no human-interest stories in the common meaning of the term. While his tales often shed light on the human predicament, he seldom develops an individual personality with whom the reader can empathize; and only rarely can we feel any sentimental attachment to his protagonists. A possible exception to the general rule may be seen in the figure of Jaromir Hladík, the central character of "El milagro secreto." The story takes place in Prague during World War II. Hladík, a scholar and author of works dealing with Jewish philosophy, has been arrested by the Nazis and sentenced to death. His crimes are nothing more than his Jewish blood and the signing of a protest against the German occupation. Having presented these basic facts, Borges describes in some detail Hladík's literary interests: not only is he a writer of scholarly works, but he is a poet and dramatist as well.[90] His current project, a drama in verse which he had hoped would be his masterpiece, was at the time of his arrest, only partially completed, though its main features were all sketched out in his mind. Its rather Borgesian, cyclical plot need not concern us; what is important is Hladík's intense desire to finish it before he dies. The night before he is to face the ignominy of the Nazi firing squad he prays to God—"to whom the centuries and time belong" ("de quien son los siglos y el tiempo")[91] to be granted a year in which to complete his project. The next morning, March 29, 1943, at precisely 8:44 he is taken out to the barracks wall. His execution is scheduled for nine o'clock sharp.

Borges etches the scene in fine detail: "Someone pointed out that the wall was going to be stained with blood; the victim was

ordered to step forward a few paces. Incongruously, this re-
minded Hladík of the fumbling preparations of photographers"
("Alguien temió que la pared quedara maculada de sangre; entonces le ordenaron al reo que avanzara unos pasos. Hladík, ab-
surdamente, recordó las vacilaciones preliminares de los fotógra-
fos").[92] Note this last detail: a very ordinary comparison—one
which is in the experience of any reader—drives home the horror
of the scene with chilling fidelity. The guns converge on Hladík,
and the sergeant raises his arm to signal the squad to fire, but at
this instant Hladík sees the world before him "freeze." The wind
stops; the soldiers are motionless; a bee in the courtyard casts "an
unchanging shadow." Hladík himself is paralyzed: only his mind
is active. He feels no fatigue and even falls asleep. Upon awakening, the scene before him remains frozen exactly as it was. After a
while he realizes that God has granted his request. Overcome with
gratitude he begins his year's work: the composition of the remaining portions of his drama. Using only his memory, he lovingly and meticulously revises and reworks the last two acts of his
masterpiece. Finally, "He had only the problem of a single phrase.
He found it . . . He opened his mouth in a maddened cry,
moved his face, dropped under the quadruple blast" ("no le fal-
taba ya resolver sino un solo epíteto. Lo encontró . . . Inició un
grito enloquecido, movió la cara, la cuádruple descarga lo der-
ribó").[93] In the last sentence Borges notes that "Jaromir Hladík
died on March 29, at 9:02 A.M." ("Jaromir Hladík murió el vein-
tinueve de marzo, a las nueve y dos minutos de la mañana.").[94]

"El milagro secreto" presents a nearly perfect blending of
Borges' finest prose style with one of his principal philosophical
concerns, the ever-present problem of time. Moreover, in this tale
he seems to accomplish the difficult objective of successfully infus-
ing an unreal element into a very real and very specific world.
And the tale's extra attraction, a flesh-and-blood protagonist who
despite his symbolic value cannot fail to evoke our sympathy,
makes "El milagro secreto" a fitting finale to our survey of Borges'
prose fiction.

CHAPTER 5

Borges and the Critics

> "Jorge Luis Borges is a phantom, he is the great *bluff* of Argentine Literature. At times an unsophisticated young lady may perhaps find his stories acceptable. Jorge Luis Borges is a hybrid product without any great interest." [1]

BORGES is the kind of author about whom few critics are neutral. This fact is especially evident in the Spanish-speaking world where his writings have received many enthusiastic accolades as well as a number of sharp attacks. The statement above by Camilo José Cela—perhaps contemporary Spain's greatest novelist—is a good example of the negative view of Borges' work. Yet non-Hispanic critics, chiefly the North Americans and the French, have tended to praise him without reservation; and at this writing (1968) his stocks in the United States seem to be soaring.

I Argentine Criticism

The earliest comments on Borges naturally deal with him as a poet. Chiefly minor pieces—reviews of his poetry collections or brief notes—they praise him but seldom attempt any real analysis. By the early 1930's, however, Borges was becoming important enough to receive adverse criticism; and in 1933 the magazine *Megáfono*, recognizing his growing stature, conducted a poll of opinions on the rising young author.

Some fifteen contributors participated, included several men who are now counted among the most distinguished writers and critics of the Hispanic world: Amado Alonso, Eduardo Mallea, Ulíses Petit de Murat, and Enrique Anderson Imbert, among others. By this time Borges' essays had attracted almost as much attention as his poetry; and as a result the *Megáfono* writers begin to differentiate Borges the poet from Borges the prose writer. Anderson Imbert, for example, attacks Borges as a critic and essayist, though he admits that his verse is probably more praiseworthy. Leon Ostrov notes that the two activities—that of poet and critical essayist—are mutually self-destructive. In short, what one writer has called the "dichotomy" in the criticism of Borges was already becoming evident. If any generalization is possible, it would be that Borges comes off best as a poet. While the stylistic qualities of his essays are frequently praised, there appears to be no general consensus of opinion regarding the value of their content.

When the jury charged with the task of selecting the winner of the National Literary Prize for the year 1941 rejected Borges' first collection of stories, *El jardín de senderos que se bifurcan,* a host of writers and critics—especially those of his own generation—rallied round their defeated comrade in a remarkable show of solidarity. Their outrage found expression in the pages of *Sur,* at the time only a decade old, but well on its way to becoming one of the Hispanic world's truly great literary magazines.[2] Borges'close friend and collaborator, Adolfo Bioy Casares, was as cutting as anyone in his assessment of the situation: "The commission . . . awarded the two first prizes to persons whom no one could confuse with writers." Eduardo Mallea, the rising novelist of the generation, was especially eloquent in his praise, comparing Borges' prose to that of Domingo Faustino Sarmiento. Luis E. Soto emphasized Borges essential *criollismo,* while the highly respected Dominican critic, Pedro Henríquez Ureña, underscored Borges' originality in what has become a famous statement: "There may be those who think that Borges is original because he proposes to be. I think quite the contrary: Borges would be original even when he might propose not to be." And Amado Alonso, in describing Borges' literary language, coined a phrase as memorable as it is untranslatable: "un estilo tan estilo" ("a style so style"). Though all the contributors seem to agree that the award should have gone to him, several indicate that their support of Borges was not without reservations. The essayist and philosopher, Francisco Romero, confined his remarks to a rather brief statement in which he merely expresses "surprise" at the jury's decision. Aníbal Sánchez Reulet states flatly, "I take issue with Borges," but he does recognize the quality of his writing and his basic Argentinity. Even Amado Alonso, so effusive in his praise of Borges' style, points out his aloofness, his apparent lack of involvement in the real world. Yet Alonso softens this comment by adding—as others have done since—that Borges' fiction contains an element of "satire of the social reality."

Few writers differ as much as Borges and his compatriot Ernesto Sábato. Some twelve years Borges' junior, Sábato, to use a well-worn term, is a "committed" writer; he appears to be intensely involved in his writing, sociopolitical considerations are frequently present in his work, and he is deeply interested in the realm of the erotic. His two novels, *El túnel* (1948) and the ponderous *Sobre héroes y tumbas* (1962), are often linked with literary existentialism. When Borges published his second collection of stories, the celebrated *Ficciones* (1944), Sábato wrote a sharply critical review of the book in *Sur*.[3] The ideas expressed in this piece have since become classical statements of the anti-Borges position. Sábato first attacks Borges' overt use of literary sources for his fiction: he dismisses these as "underlying fossils." He then points out Borges' tendency to reshuffle the same limited number of ideas—a literary trait that was apparent even as early as 1945: "The influence that Borges has kept on having on Borges seems insuperable. Will he be condemmed from now on to plagiarize himself?" Borges' lack of seriousness also irritates Sábato. Two points which he makes in this regard are probably true: that Borges' fantasies do not have the nightmarish involvement found in Kafka and that Borges' interest in theological matters is merely "a game of a non-believer." Sábato also attacks Borges' over-all views on fiction: his fondness for the "geometrization" of narrative, and his critique of the psychological novel. Yet, like a number of others who have reservations about Borges' prose, Sábato expresses considerable respect for his poetry, and thus he concludes his article with a rich statement that sums up the ambivalence in his attitude: "I see you Borges above all as a Great Poet. And afterward, thus: arbitrary, brilliant, tender, a watchmaker, great, triumphant, daring, timid, a failure, magnificent, unhappy, limited, infantile, and immortal."

Adolfo Prieto approaches Borges' work from the viewpoint of a different generation and with a radically different concept of the relationship between writers and the world. "Borges is a writer for the writers of *his* generation" is the *leitmotiv* running through Prieto's study. The younger men of letters, he claims, can't even "react against" Borges. One of the clearest statements of his opinion appears early in his book: "Detective fiction and fantasy suffer from the same defects . . . as the novel of chivalry and the pastoral novel. These defects spring basically from the complete gratuity of these genres, from their absolute forgetting of man, from their schematization of reality. . . ." [4]

Yet even as a writer of fantasy, Borges is found lacking. Prieto concentrates his attack on the story "El Aleph," a choice which is certainly revealing. As we saw this particular tale is well spiced with Borgesian humor: though it might seem rather inept if it is taken with complete seriousness. As might be expected, Prieto does exactly this. He objects most of all to what he calls "the direct presentation" of the fantastic. He feels that Borges fails in not preparing the reader for the series of "ineffable" events which follow once the author descends into Carlos Argentino's basement. "Everything is possible in the world of fantasy, provided we are captured by it. . . . If our feet remain on the ground, the attempt fails. . . . The most difficult task . . . for the acutely imaginative artist is to transform the earthbound spectator into a fantastic spectator, to stamp his passport to a world different from ours. . . . The realm of the fantastic, viewed from the outside . . . is simply absurd." [5] Prieto's objections, taken in the general sense, are justified. Their application to this story, however, is not —unless we, like the critic, assume a dead seriousness which the tale lacks. In reviewing the titles of the stories that Prieto chooses for praise or condemnation, one is struck by his omissions. [6] His criteria for good fantasy might well have been applied, for example, to "Las ruinas circulares." Yet he does not discuss this magnificent story at all. Could this omission be the result of some deliberate card-stacking against Borges?

The same year in which Prieto's book appeared (1954) Jorge Abelardo Ramos published a highly polemical—and highly questionable—volume titled *Crisis y resurrección de la literatura Argentina*. In it he attacks a heterogeneous group of Argentine writers, Borges included. Ramos' views cannot be assessed in a vacuum: their author is a man of strong opinions (a *peronista* and heterodox Marxist) whose politics unquestionably color his literary criticism. Ramos' main point is that Argentina is still a semicolonial state and that any writer who does not contribute to the creation of a vigorous national literature, is, in a sense, an agent of the foreign devils.

The criticisms of Ramos and Prieto, despite the irresponsibility of the former and the incompleteness of the latter, were echoed in the work of an entire group of young intellectuals. These men— the generation of the Parricides, as one critic has termed them[7]— were attempting to reassess writers of Borges' generation who had become the acknowledged literary leaders of the nation. Their activity, significantly, centers around the year 1955—the date of Perón's overthrow. With few exceptions they follow the general lines of anti-Borges criticism suggested by Prieto, who was actually a member of the group: to a lesser extent, they accepted Ramos' views. But Borges' defenders were not silent. Two books, both by younger critics, apppeared the same year.

The first of these, José Luis Ríos Patrón's *Jorge Luis Borges*, takes as its point of departure the idea that Borges is not "ahuman," aloof, or divorced from reality: "we must admit that all of Borges' work is not only profoundly human, but is characterized by a desperate certainty of the futility of our efforts to extricate ourselves from the chaos into which we have been cast." [8] In the second work, co-authors Marcial Tamayo and Adolfo Ruiz-Díaz concentrate their efforts on a close analysis of the better-known prose fiction of Borges rather than on a general view of his total literary production. Their attitude is not particularly defensive or polemical: obviously they admire Borges' work greatly, but they choose to describe, explain, and recount rather than propagandize.

César Fernández Moreno's over-all assessment of Borges, as seen in his *Esquema de Borges* (1957), lies somewhere between the extremes of extravagant praise and wholesale rejection. He holds that Borges should not be required to be something which he is not; and he maintains that Borges is neither the "foreign agent" of some critics nor the devoted *criollista* of others. Rather, he is "a premature phenomenon if our culture." Moreover, Fernández Moreno believes that his work cannot be considered "useless," as Prieto had claimed. Fernández concludes his slender volume by affirming that say what one will about him, "the very presence of Borges among us has constituted since 1921 a call to effort, an invitation to breathe the air of a certain superior and rarified culture." [9]

Ana María Barrenechea's *La expresión de la irrealidad en la obra de Jorge Luis Borges* (1957) is the culmination of several years' work. To date it is the most scholarly study on Borges to have appeared. The book, as its title suggests, is limited to the notion of "irreality," especially in Borges' prose fiction. The author states clearly in her conclusion that this is only one of many aspects of his writings and to interpret him solely on the basis of his cultivation of "irreality" might lead to "a purely negative and false idea of Borges' work." Barrenechea's fundamental attitude toward Borges is one of great admiration, though she does not attempt to write literary propaganda in his behalf. One gets the impression that she considers Borges quite above the polemic which others have created about his work. Obviously she feels sufficiently convinced of his greatness to avoid the defensiveness found in a number of other pro-Borges critics.

One final observation: Barrenechea, like many others, puts little emphasis on the high humor found so frequently in Borges' writing. One wishes that a chapter of her book might have been "Reality as a Bad Joke" or, even better, "The Writer as Jester." The slighting of the humor in Borges gives Barrenechea's general remarks on his work a kind of solemnity and anguished seriousness which appears out of keeping with his basic literary personality. Note, for example, the following: "To undermine the reader's belief in the concreteness of life, Borges attacks those fundamental concepts on which the security of living itself is founded: the universe, personality, and time. The universe is converted into a meaningless chaos abandoned to chance or ruled by inhuman gods. . . ."[10] Or, from Barrenechea's concluding statements, "Borges is an admirable writer pledged to destroy reality and convert Man into a shadow. The process of dissolution of concepts on which Man's belief in the concreteness of his life is founded . . . has been analyzed. Also viewed here have been the anguishing presence of the Infinite and the disintegration of the substantial. . . ."[11]

Rafael Gutiérrez Girardot's *Jorge Luis Borges, Ensayo de interpretación* (1959) fills in some of the gaps in Barrenechea's study and also presents Borges' literary personality in a slightly different light. Yet this book is, as its title indicates, more of an interpretive essay than a detailed study. Gutiérrez Girardot makes no thoroughgoing thematic analysis of Borges' work nor does he attempt to show interrelationships between the various genres.

Argentine studies on Borges have continued to appear. Isaac

Wolberg's *Jorge Luis Borges* (1961) is little more than an essay in which the author takes great pains to demonstrate Borges' deep-rooted Argentinity. His enthusiasm is indicated by the fact that he predicts that Borges will eventually receive a Nobel Prize. Alicia Jurado's *Genio y figura de Jorge Luis Borges* (1964) is an unpretentious but extremely informative book on Borges the person as well as Borges the author: Jurado is a good friend who approaches his work with warmth and enthusiasm, but not with awe. As a result, her book, though certainly not a definitive study, is rich in insights. Señora Jurado is well aware of Borges' sense of humor, she is sensitive to his essentially retiring personality, and most important, she accepts him for what he is.

II *International Criticism*

French interest in Borges may be seen first among the refugees who resided in Buenos Aires during the war, and shortly afterward it is evidenced in the French translations of his prose. The French are probably more responsible for the "internationalization" of Borges than are any other non-Argentine people; though a real appreciation of his work, at least in academic circles, has been evident in the United States since the late 1940's. It should also be noted that an Italian translation of *El Aleph* appeared in 1954, while in the same year, several of his major stories were published in German. Yet it was the French who first produced book-length translations of his work and these by a major publishing firm, Gallimard. By 1957 a very substantial portion of his best stories and essays were available to French readers. The Prix Formentor—the International Publishers' Prize—awarded him in Paris in 1961, firmly established his international position.[12] It was only after this date that book-length translations of his work appeared in English, and that non-academic literary circles in this country began to notice him.

Along with the Argentinian, French, and North American interest in Borges, the Mexican critical reception merits special consideration. It will be recalled that Barrenechea's book on Borges was published in Mexico. Another book-length study, Manuel Blanco-González' *Jorge Luis Borges: Anotaciones sobre el tiempo en su obra* (1963), also appeared there. Mexican interest in Borges, however, goes back considerably earlier. In the 1940's the Argentine writer was known and admired by Alfonso Reyes, who de-

scribed Borges' distinctive fiction in his *El deslinde;* by Alí Chumacero who analyzed his poetry in the journal *Letras mexicanas;*
and by Xavier Villaurrutia who wrote a very favorable review of
Ficciones in the important literary magazine *El Hijo Pródigo.* A
marked rise in interest in Borges seems to have taken place in
Mexico since the late fifties. Leading journals such as the *Revista
Universidad de Mexico* and *La Palabra y el Hombre* have published much material on him, a good deal of which is highly polemical in character.

North American criticism on Borges has been characterized by
a steadily increasing interest on the part of specialists in Spanish
American literature, and—with the recent appearance of his work
in translation—by a growing appreciation of him in nonacademic
circles. Readers in the United States could sample Borges' works
in English as early as the late 1940's when the "little magazines"
began publishing his stories. But it was not until the major translations appeared—the Irby-Yates *Labyrinths* (1962), Anthony
Kerrigan's *Ficciones* (1962), the University of Texas' *Dreamtigers*
(1964), and Kerrigan's *Personal Anthology* (1967)—that the nonspecialists began to notice Borges.

John Updike's review of Borges' work in the *New Yorker* of
October 30, 1965 is a milestone in the American understanding
of Borges. Updike's long article is candid, sophisticated, and full
of relevancy for the North American reader. He is especially sensitive to the problems posed by the "arrival" of a previously unknown foreign writer on the international, or in this case, American literary scene. What is most interesting is that Updike sees a
real possibility that such a writer may have an important effect on
our literature. "The question is, I think, whether or not Borges'
lifework . . . can serve, in its gravely considered oddity, as any
kind of clue to the way out of the dead-end narcissism and down-
right trashiness of present American fiction." [13] Perhaps what appeals most to the reviewer is the fact that "Borges' narrative innovations spring from a clear sense of technical crisis. For all his
modesty . . . he proposes some sort of essential revision in literature itself." [14] Yet Updike concludes his introductory observations
by remarking that Borges "seems to be the man for whom literature has no future," a casual statement which may well be an important clue to Borges' current vogue. Throughout his article Updike hits the mark: he sees the essential differences between

Borges and Kafka with great clarity; his interpretations of the Borgesian attitudes toward eroticism and "femaleness" are well taken; finally, his summation of Borges' thoughts on the novel is especially penetrating: "Certainly the traditional novel as a transparent imitation of human circumstances has 'a distracted or tired air.' Ironic and blasphemous as Borges' hidden message may seem, the texture and method of his creations . . . answer to a deep need in contemporary literary art—the need to confess the fact of artifice." [15]

A number of recent articles, reviews, interviews, and reprints of Borges' work attest his growing stature in North American literary circles. John Ashberry's enthusiastic review of Borges' *Personal Anthology* in the *New York Times Book Review* in April, 1967, is a case in point, while *Time* magazine's book editor joined the chorus of praise with a review that will, no doubt, further endear the publication to Latin American readers: "Argentina has no national literature, but it has produced a literary mind that is as mysterious and elusive as the fretted shadows on the moonlit grass." [16]

Borges' influence on other creative writers is, and will be, difficult to assess. This is so because, paradoxically, he is both unoriginal and inimitable. Other writers may admire his work and be stimulated by it: they may "reflect" it in a chance phrase, and literary joke, or a vague parallel. For example, Vladimir Nabokov's fondness for Borges' work may be exactly documented.[17] Readers who are familiar with the Russian-American writer's *Pale Fire*—a novel built around the detailed literary discussion of a cyclical and imagined poem—may recognize in it an echo of Borgesian art. The young North American novelist John Barth is another writer who has expressed a great attraction for Borges' fiction. Barth, however, has discussed this attraction in considerable detail. His provocative article, "The Literature of Exhaustion," will conclude our view of Borges and the critics.

Writing in the summer of 1967, Barth sees the current state of the arts very clearly and is very much disturbed by what he sees. Like Updike, he views contemporary art as having reached a dead end, or a point of no return. Pop art, "happenings," the "intermedia" arts, and the like have at their roots a "tendency to eliminate not only the traditional audience . . . but also the most traditional notion of the artist: the Aristotelian conscious agent who achieves with technique and cunning the artistic effect; in other words, one endowed with uncommon talent, who has moreover developed and disciplined that endowment into virtuosity." [18] Barth's ideas on contemporaneity in art form the next basic step in his argument: it is essential, he feels, for a good literary work to be "technically up-to-date": "A good many current novelists write turn-of-the-century-type novels, only in more or less mid-twentieth-century language and about contemporary people and topics; this makes them considerably less interesting (to me) than excellent writers who are also technically contemporary: Joyce and Kafka, for instance, in their time, and in ours, Samuel Becket and Jorge Luis Borges." [19] Borges, Barth claims, illustrates the third of three categories of writers: in the first group are those that write as if the twentieth century didn't even exist; in the second category are the very inspired, very contemporary-minded but essentially technique-less "pop" artists; and in the third group are those few outstanding writers who are "hip . . . but who manage nonetheless to speak eloquently and memorably to our still-human hearts and conditions, as the great artists have always done." [20]

One of the hallmarks of our times, Barth goes on to say, is the fact that a sense of "ultimacies" pervades everything from theology to weaponry. Borges, he notes, is not only *aware* of esthetic ultimacies, but he *uses* them in his literature. A study such as "Pierre Menard, autor del Quijote" illustrates perfectly this technique of pushing an esthetic idea to the ultimate point. It is done with ironic intent by an author "quite aware of where we've been and where we are": it constitutes an "ironic comment on the genre [i.e., the novel] and the history of art." Carrying the idea a bit further, it suggests "the difficulty, perhaps the unnecessity, of writing original works of literature." This notion is further underscored in Barth's article when he discusses "Tlön, Uqbar, Orbis Tertius," and again when he analyzes Borges' fascination for the *regressus in infinitum*—"an image of the exhaustion, or attempted exhaustion, of possibilities. . . ." [21] For the "exhaustion of possibilities," like the "felt ultimacies" in contemporary life, leads toward an "intellectual dead-end." Barth relates Borges' ideas on the impossibility (or at least the difficulty) of "originality in literature" to the same theme; that is, to the "used-upness of certain forms or exhaustion of certain possibilities." Although Barth does not say that Borges writes in a Baroque manner, he does attribute a Baroque "intellectuality" to him—another way of saying that his is a literature of exhausted possibilities, granting that we equate the Baroque with the exhaustion of the "possibilities of novelty."

Barth concludes his remarks by examining the idea of the labyrinth, often considered the most basic of Borgesian images. "A labyrinth '. . . is a place in which, ideally, all the possibilities of choice . . . are embodied . . . and must be exhausted before one reaches the heart." Borges' function ("a heroic enterprise, with salvation as its object") is to go "through the maze to the accomplishment of his work." To do this requires *"very special gifts"* which, in Barth's view, Borges clearly possesses. Barth's description of the process involves some fine-spun reasoning: like Theseus, who has Ariadne's thread to guide him through the labyrinth, Borges "need not rehearse its [the labyrinth's] possibilities to exhaustion";[22] with his special talents he only needs to be aware of the infinitude of possibilities to perform his heroic task successfully.

III   *Conclusion: Borges and the State of Literature*

The foregoing review of critical opinion on Borges has been presented not merely to show the status of Borgesian criticism here and abroad but to demonstrate that Borges represents different things to different people. His is a unique case: that of a writer whose first fifty years have been spent within an intellectual and literary environment which—rightfully or wrongfully—has been relegated to a peripheral or secondary position with respect to the main current of the Western tradition, but whose last fifteen years have been spent as a member of a small group of internationally respected literary masters. To Argentine writers of his own generation much of Borges is a known quantity: he is the contemporary of Mallea, Martínez Estrada, and Güiraldes who abandoned the *martinfierristas*, the *barrios* of Buenos Aires, and the literary polemics of the 1920's to create a strange and perhaps alien literature which has succeeded in attracting the attention of Paris and New York. To the present-day French or North American reader he is an author who, in a sense, only began writing in the late 1940's or 1950's: he seems to be part of a new literary wave the crest of which he shares with men like Nabokov, Beckett, Robbe-Grillet, and perhaps John Barth. To younger Argen-

tines and other Latin Americans of the generation which reached
maturity just after World War II, Borges is especially perplexing:
there is so much about his work that is attractive, and there is the
undeniable fact that he has shown the literary world that Hispanic America can produce first-rate writers; yet these men cannot
afford the luxury of his cool detachment and his cosmopolitanism.
"If Borges were French or Czech," Ernesto Sábato wrote in 1945,
"we would all be reading him in bad translations." [23] The remark is
significant and is still valid today. Borges' cultivation of "artifice"
—to use John Updike's very appropriate term—can be accepted
in the work of a foreign writer, but many Latin Americans hold
that their own writers have an obligation to pursue matters which
bear more directly on the real world—especially *their* real world.
This attitude, which goes beyond mere questions of cultural nationalism or politics, cannot be explored here, yet is one which
almost always lies just below the surface of any discussion of Hispanic American letters.

Those who seek answers to philosophical or psychological questions in literature will have difficulty in appreciating Borges. Despite his tremendous interest in philosophy, metaphysics, and theology, he is, to use his own word, an anachronism. Few people
today can generate any serious concern over the problems raised
by Berkeleyan idealism, the Gnostics, or the refutation of time.
For Borges these matters are essentially a means toward literary
ends. To consider them as anything more is to read him incor-
rectly. Similarly, literary attempts at psychological reality (and
perhaps even the attempts of psychiatrists) are, in Borges' view,
doomed to failure. They are, moreover, intellectually dishonest
monuments to human vanity. What Borges appears to tell us is
that the infinite complexity of a single human being (and of the
entire universe) is such that if we would preserve at least a degree
of honesty, we must admit the fact of artifice.

Yet Borges in his own way may have something very important
to say about the real world. A number of critics have pointed out
the humor and especially the irony in his work. There is, I think,
an underlying Borgesian irony which serves on the one hand to
lend coherence to all his work, and on the other, to demonstrate
that the attempt to separate the "real" and "literary" realms is
pointless. Borges holds that language and literature (a specially
organized category of language) form an arbitrary system of sym-

bols which we use to describe something that lies beyond our ken —"real reality." Language and literature are then nothing more than a vast metaphor which stands for an unknown quantity. There is something quite ironical—even quite funny—about people who fail to realize this and who foolishly attempt to see more than the accessible side of this metaphor.

It is not surprising, then, that Borges should often be called a writer's writer. His is a world of literature, and those who are not at least moderately "literary" in their tastes and background will find much of his work dull—except perhaps for those stories where the sheer plot interest might carry them along. Yet as a literary man—not as a philosopher or commentator upon the present state of human affairs—he is superb. Despite his occasional remarks to the effect that he is lazy, he is at heart a craftsman. The respect for work well done permeates his writings and is one of his most cherished values. Timid and daring, sophisticated and childish, dazzling and erudite, yet essentially humble, a writer who has sought to refute time, historical development, and "novelty," Borges is ironically held up as the quintessence of literary contemporaneity. Why should this be so?

Borges' writing—and that of people like him—invites us to ask just what the decades of naturalism, psychologism, social protest, and "committed" literature have produced. A conservative, and in this sense Borges is very conservative, might reply that writing of this kind has neither improved the state of letters nor the state of humanity. *If* this is so, then authors might just as well not deceive themselves or flatter their egos; rather, they should unpretentiously tend their vineyards and devote themselves to their craft. By doing so they may even perform some valuable services: they may stand as examples to a world dangerously intoxicated with vanity; certainly, they will help to transcend those "exhausted possibilities" which seem to characterize contemporary letters.

Notes and References

Chapter One

1. Alicia Jurado, *Genio y figura de Jorge Luis Borges* (Buenos Aires, 1964), p. 51.
2. Cited by Gloria Videla, *El ultraísmo* (Madrid, 1963), p. 143.
3. *Obra poética* (Buenos Aires, 1964), p. 39.
4. *Otras inquisiciones* (Buenos Aires, 1960), p. 53.
5. Cited by Videla, p. 201.
6. *Nosotros*, XV, No. 151 (Dec. 1921), 466–471.
7. *Macedonio Fernández.* (Buenos Aires, 1961), p. 20.
8. *Ibid.*
9. Jurado, p. 41.
10. *Ibid.*, p. 42. See also the recent interview with Ronald Christ, "The Art of Fiction: Jorge Luis Borges," *Paris Review*, No. 40 (Winter–Spring 1967), 116–64.
11. The prize was shared with Samuel Beckett, since there was a tie in the competition.
12. Jurado, p. 20.
13. James E. Irby, "Encuentro con Borges," *Revista Universidad de México*, XVI, No. 10 (June 1962), 4.
14. "Entretien avec Gloria Alcorta," *L'Herne*, 1964, 404–8.

Chapter Two

1. "Ultraísmo," *Nosotros*, XV, No. 151 (Dec. 1921), 466–71.
2. Borges (or his editors) has omitted several of the poems from later editions. In the 1958 Emecé edition of *Poemas* there are 36 pieces in the *Fervor de Buenos Aires* and in the 1964 *Obra poética*, only 35.
3. *Obra poética* (Buenos Aires, 1964), p. 17. Unless noted otherwise, succeeding references are to this edition.
4. *Ibid.*, p. 23.
5. *Ibid.*, p. 26.
6. *Ibid.*, p. 43.
7. *Ibid.*, p. 47.
8. *Ibid.*, p. 30.
9. *Ibid.*, p. 34.

10. *Ibid.*, p. 57.

11. *Ibid.*, p. 17.

12. *Ibid.*, p. 62.

13. *Ibid.*, p. 30. In the original edition (1923), the word *parra* in the poem's last line is *alero* ("eaves").

14. *Ibid.*, p. 56.

15. *Ibid.*

16. *Ibid.*, p. 58.

17. *Ibid.*, p. 53.

18. *Ibid.*, p. 54.

19. *Ibid.*, p. 20.

20. *Ibid.*, p. 47.

21. *Ibid.*, p. 48.

22. *Ibid.*

23. *Ibid.*, p. 49.

24. *Ibid.*, p. 25.

25. *Poemas: 1923–1958* (Buenos Aires, 1958), p. 60. This line appears as cited in the 1958 and earlier editions of the collection. In the 1964 edition a variant appears: "es como un remanso en la sombra" (p. 62).

26. *Obra poética*, p. 67.

27. *Ibid.*, p. 32.

28. *Ibid.*

29. *Ibid.*, p. 33.

30. *Ibid.*, p. 27.

31. *Ibid.*, p. 28.

32. A good example of the poetry supressed in later editions is "Llamarada." The piece is actually a prose-poem, quite confessional, and even rather erotic. Note the line, "deseando . . . perdernos en las culminaciones carnales . . ."

33. *Obra poética*, p. 64.

34. *Luna de enfrente* (Buenos Aires, 1925), p. 7.

35. *Poemas: 1923–1958*, p. 82. This verse is omitted from the poem in the 1964 *Obra poética*.

36. *Obra poética*, p. 77.

37. *Ibid.*, p. 76.

38. *Ibid.*, p. 77.

39. *Ibid.*, p. 78.

40. "Contestación a la encuesta sobre la nueva generación literaria," *Nosotros*, XVII, No. 168 (May 1923), 16–17.

41. *Obra poética*, p. 98.

42. *Ibid.*, p. 88.

43. *Ibid.*, p. 80.

44. Two good examples of poems of this type in the original edition

are "La vuelta a Buenos Aires" and "Patrias"; both are omitted from more recent editions.

45. *Obra poética*, p. 107.
46. *Ibid.*, p. 122.
47. *Ibid.*, pp. 125–26.
48. *Ibid.*, p. 122.
49. *Ibid.*, pp. 113–14.
50. *Ibid.*, p. 142.
51. *Ibid.*, pp. 140–41.
52. *Ibid.*, pp. 142–43.
53. *Ibid.*, p. 138.
54. *Ibid.*, pp. 144–45.
55. *Ibid.*, p. 147.
56. See Ana María Barrenechea, *Borges the Labyrinth Maker* (New York, 1965), p. 17.
57. *Obra poética*, p. 149.
58. Barrenechea, p. 17.
59. *Obra poética*, pp. 157–58.
60. *Ibid.*, p. 177.
61. *Ibid.*, p. 176.
62. *Ibid.*, pp. 264–65.
63. *Ibid.*
64. *Ibid.*, p. 258.
65. Cited by Ana María Barrenechea in *La expresión de la irrealidad en la obra de Jorge Luis Borges* (México, 1957), p. 10. The English translation appears in Barrenechea's *Borges the Labyrinth Maker*, p. 17.
66. *Obra poética*, p. 224. English translation by Harold Morland in *Dreamtigers* (Austin, 1964), p. 89.

Chapter Three

1. For details regarding exact dates of publication for individual essays see the bibliography to Ana María Barrenechea's *La expresión de la irrealidad en la obra de Jorge Luis Borges* (México, 1957), pp. 145–64.
2. In some cases the Emecé editions are modified second editions of original titles, in other cases—*Otras inquisiciones,* for example—the Emecé is in fact an original collection. For clarification, see: "Bibliography," pp. 161–62.
3. See above, Chapter 2, pp. 18–19.
4. *Inquisiciones* (Buenos Aires, 1925), pp. 153–59.
5. *Ibid.*, pp. 139–45.
6. *Ibid.*, pp. 26–29.
7. *Ibid.*, pp. 39–45.

8. *Ibid.*, p. 37.

9. *Ibid.*, p. 74.

10. *Ibid.*, p. 19.

11. *Ibid.*, p. 80.

12. *Ibid.*, p. 62.

13. For further information on the life and works of Fernández, see Borges' own *Macedonio Fernández* (Buenos Aires, 1961).

14. *Inquisiciones*, p. 91.

15. *Ibid.*, pp. 114–15.

16. *El tamaño de mi esperanza* (Buenos Aires, 1926), p. 5.

17. *Ibid.*, pp. 9–10.

18. See "El escritor argentino y la tradición," in *Discusión* (Buenos Aires, 1957), p. 156.

19. *El tamaño de mi esperanza*, p. 100.

20. *Ibid.*, pp. 45–46. Cf. *Inquisiciones*, pp. 65–66.

21. *El tamaño de mi esperanza*, p. 154.

22. "Prólogo," *El idioma de los argentinos* (Buenos Aires, 1928).

23. *El idioma de los argentinos*, pp. 170ff. Cf. *El tamaño de mi esperanza*, pp. 45–46 and *Inquisiciones*, pp. 65–66.

24. *El idioma de los argentinos*, p. 56.

25. *Ibid.*, p. 57.

26. *Ibid.*, p. 68.

27. *Ibid.*, p. 45.

28. *Ibid.*, pp. 101–2.

29. *Ibid.*, p. 102.

30. *Ibid.*, pp. 147–48.

31. *Evaristo Carriego* (Buenos Aires, 1955), p. 38.

32. *Ibid.*, p. 33.

33. *Discusión* (Buenos Aires, 1932), p. 9.

34. *Ibid.*, p. 12.

35. For early indications of this interest, see the poem "Amanecer" in the *Fervor de Buenos Aires* and the essay "Canción del barrio" in *Evaristo Carriego*.

36. *Discusión* (Buenos Aires, 1957), p. 66. Unless otherwise noted, succeeding references to this collection will be to this edition.

37. *Ibid.*, p. 58.

38. "Avatares de la tortuga," *Otras inquisiciones* (Buenos Aires, 1952), p. 129. The particular essay is dated 1939.

39. *Discusión*, p. 120.

40. *Ibid.*, p. 108.

41. *Ibid.*, p. 88.

42. *Ibid.*, p. 90.

43. *Ibid.*, p. 91.

44. *Historia de la eternidad* (Buenos Aires, 1953), pp. 20–21.

45. *Ibid.,* p. 37.

46. "Nueva refutación del tiempo," in *Otras inquisiciones* (Buenos Aires, 1960), p. 235. Though the essay was published as a booklet in 1947, it has been included as the final essay in the 1960 edition of *Otras inquisiciones,* to which my quotations refer.

47. *Otras inquisiciones,* p. 237.

48. *Ibid.*

49. *Ibid.,* p. 243–44.

50. *Ibid.,* p. 236.

51. *Ibid.,* p. 256. The English translation is by James E. Irby in *Labyrinths* (New York, 1962), pp. 233–34.

52. "Libros y autores extranjeros. Guía de lectores," *Revista Hogar,* Jan. 22, 1937, p. 30.

53. "La última invención de Hugh Walpole," *La Nación,* Jan. 10, 1943.

54. *Otras inquisiciones,* p. 79.

55. *Ibid.,* pp. 68–69.

56. *Ibid.,* pp. 220–21. Translation by Irby in *Labyrinths,* p. 216.

57. *Discusión,* p. 142. Note that this item is not included in *Otras inquisiciones.* Since its theme is germane to the discussion of Borges' ideas on the novel, it has been included at this point.

58. *Otras inquisiciones,* p. 40.

59. *Ibid.,* pp. 148–49.

60. *Ibid.,* p. 156.

61. *Ibid.,* p. 133.

62. *Ibid.,* p. 175.

63. James E. Irby, "Introduction" to *Labyrinths* (New York, 1962), p. xxii.

64. Miguel Enguídanos, "Introduction" to *Dreamtigers* (Austin, 1964), p. 16.

65. Note that in contrast to many of the compositions in *El hacedor,* "Dreamtigers" was written rather early in Borges' career. It appeared first in the review *Crítica* in 1934.

66. *El hacedor* (Buenos Aires, 1960), p. 51.

Chapter Four

1. Cited by Ronald Christ in "The Art of Fiction: Jorge Luis Borges," *Paris Review,* No. 40 (Winter–Spring 1967), 124.

2. *Historia universal de la infamia* (Buenos Aires, 1954), p. 10.

3. Cited by Christ, p. 124.

4. *Ficciones* (Buenos Aires, 1956), p. 125. English translation by Irby, *Labyrinths,* p. 65. References to Irby's translation in the following notes are in parenthesis.

5. *Ibid.,* p. 127. (Irby, p. 66.)

6. *Ibid.*, p. 126. (Irby, p. 66.)
7. *Ibid.*, p. 49. (Irby, p. 39.)
8. *Ibid.*, p. 50. (Irby, p. 39.)
9. *Ibid.*, p. 52. (Irby, p. 41.)
10. *Ibid.*, p. 51. (Irby, pp. 40–41.)
11. *Ibid.*, p. 54. (Irby, p. 42.)
12. *Ibid.*, p. 56. (Irby, p. 44.)
13. *Ibid.*, p. 54. (Irby, p. 42.)
14. *Ibid.*, p. 55. (Irby, pp. 43–44.)
15. *Ibid.*, p. 80.
16. *Ibid.*, p. 79.
17. *Ibid.*, pp. 174–75. (Irby, p. 99.)
18. *Ibid.*, p. 175. (Irby, p. 100.)
19. *Ibid.*, p. 176. (Irby, p. 100.)
20. *Ibid.*, p. 18. (Irby, p. 7.)
21. The three helpers mentioned here are, of course very real, well-known Spanish American writers. Reyes (d. 1959) was a highly regarded Mexican essayist and humanist, Martínez Estrada (d. 1964), an Argentine poet and essayist, and Nestor Ibarra, a Franco-Argentine critic.
22. *Ficciones*, p. 20. (Irby, p. 8.)
23. *Ibid.*, p. 21. (Irby, p. 8.)
24. *Ibid.*, p. 22. (Irby, p. 9.)
25. *Ibid.* (Irby, p. 10.)
26. *Ibid.*, p. 23. (Irby, p. 10.)
27. *Ibid.*, p. 27. (Irby, p. 13.)
28. *Ibid.* (Irby, p. 13.)
29. *Ibid.*, p. 28. (Irby, p. 14.)
30. *Ibid.*, p. 30. (Irby, p. 15.)
31. *Ibid.*, p. 33. (Irby, p. 17.)
32. *Ibid.*, p. 34. (Irby, p. 18.)
33. *Ibid.*, p. 11.
34. *Ibid.*, pp. 11–12.
35. *Ibid.*, p. 39.
36. See below, Chap. 5, pp. 139–40.
37. *El Aleph* (Buenos Aires, 1949), p. 127.
38. *Ibid.*, pp. 129–30.
39. *Ibid.*, p. 135.
40. *Ibid.*, p. 138.
41. *Ibid.*, p. 139.
42. *Ibid.*
43. *Ibid.*, pp. 140–41.
44. *Ibid.*, 112–13. English translation by Dudley Fitts, in *Labyrinths*, p. 161.

45. *Ibid.,* p. 116. (Fitts, p. 164.)

46. *Ficciones,* p. 85. English translation by James E. Irby in *Labyrinths,* p. 51.

47. *Ibid.,* p. 86. (Irby, p. 52.)

48. *Ibid.*

49. *Ibid.,* p. 95. (Irby, p. 58.)

50. *Ibid.,* p. 89. (Irby, p. 54.)

51. A curious slip here—perhaps intentional—in that Borges uses a dieresis over the *o.* This would naturally increase the total number of possibilities in the Library, since Borges specifically states that only the comma, period, space and lower-case letters constitute its orthographic symbols! See *Ficciones,* p. 87n.

52. *Ficciones,* p. 94. (Irby, p. 57.)

53. *Ibid.,* p. 91. (Irby, p. 55.)

54. *Ibid.,* p. 68. English translation by John M. Fein in *Labyrinths,* p. 30.

55. *Ibid.,* p. 71. (Fein, p. 32.)

56. *Ibid.,* p. 73. (Fein, p. 34.)

57. *Ibid.,* p. 74. (Fein, p. 35.)

58. *Ibid.,* p. 75. (Fein, p. 35.)

59. *Ibid.,* p. 137. English translation by James E. Irby in *Labyrinths,* p. 72.

60. *Ficciones,* p. 129. English translation by Donald A. Yates in *Labyrinths,* p. 67.

61. *Ficciones,* p. 131. (Yates, p. 68.)

62. *Ibid.,* p. 135. (Yates, p. 71.)

63. *Ibid.*

64. *Ibid.,* p. 130. (Yates, p. 68.)

65. *Ibid.*

66. *Ibid.,* p. 133. (Yates, p. 70.)

67. *Ibid.,* p. 59. English translation by James E. Irby in *Labyrinths,* p. 45.

68. *Ibid.*

69. *Ibid.,* p. 60. (Irby, p. 46.)

70. *Ibid.,* p. 62. (Irby, p. 47.)

71. *Ibid.,* p. 63. (Irby, p. 48.)

72. *Ibid.,* p. 64. (Irby. p. 48.)

73. *Ibid.* (Irby, p. 49.)

74. *Ibid.,* p. 65. (Irby, p. 50.)

75. *Ibid.,* p. 66. (Irby, p. 50.)

76. *Ibid.,* p. 153. English translation by Donald A. Yates in *Labyrinths,* p. 83.

77. *Ibid.,* p. 157. (Yates, p. 86.)

78. Borges' penchant for creating an interlocking system of apoc-

ryphal names is well illustrated here: "Tres versiones de Judas" (*Ficciones,* pp. 169–76) centers about the life and works of a fictitious scholar, Nils *Runeberg.* With two Runebergs in the same collection, the reader begins to assume their reality. Note also the meaning of "rune," an old Scandinavian word denoting "a secret, a mystery" and by extension, a letter of the alphabet or a cipher.

79. *Ficciones,* p. 99. English translation by Donald A. Yates in *Labyrinths,* p. 21.

80. *Ficciones,* p. 111. (Yates, p. 29.)

81. *Ibid.,* p. 109. (Yates, p. 28.)

82. *El Aleph,* p. 11. English translation by James E. Irby in *Labyrinths,* p. 108.

83. *El Aleph,* p. 15. (Irby, pp. 110–11.)

84. *Ibid.,* p. 19. (Irby, p. 113.)

85. *Ibid.,* p. 19. (Irby, p. 113.)

86. *Ibid.,* p. 21. (Irby, p. 115.)

87. *Ibid.,* p. 25. (Irby, p. 117.)

88. *Ibid.,* p. 26. (Irby, p. 118.)

89. *Ibid.,* p. 68. English translation by Donald A. Yates in *Labyrinths,* p. 137.

90. Another good illustration of Borges' interlocking apocrypha may be seen here. In a footnote to Nils Runeberg's theological studies (see "Tres versiones de Judas," *Ficciones,* p. 174n.), Borges cites one of Hladík's scholarly works!

91. *Ficciones,* p. 164. English translation by Harriet de Onís in *Labyrinths,* p. 92.

92. *Ibid.,* p. 165. (de Onís, p. 93.)

93. *Ibid.,* p. 167. (de Onís, p. 94.)

94. *Ibid.*

Chapter Five

1. Camilo José Cela, "Buenos Aires o un mar sin orillas," *Indice,* No. 59 (Jan. 30, 1953), p. 2.

2. See "Desagravio a Borges," *Sur,* No. 94 (July 1942), pp. 7–34.

3. Ernesto Sábato, "Los relatos de Jorge Luis Borges," *Sur,* No. 125 (March 1945), pp. 69–75.

4. *Borges y la nueva generación* (Buenos Aires, 1954), p. 18.

5. *Ibid.,* pp. 70–71.

6. A more balanced critic, Emir Rodríguez Monegal, has observed that Prieto appears to have read "only 10 per cent" of Borges' work. See Rodríguez Monegal's *El juicio de los parricidas* (Buenos Aires, 1956), p. 70.

7. See Rodríguez Monegal, *El juicio de los parricidas.*

8. José Luis Ríos Patrón, *Jorge Luis Borges* (Buenos Aires, 1955), p. 29.

9. César Fernández Moreno, *Esquema de Borges* (Buenos Aires, 1957), p. 43.

10. *Borges The Labyrinth Maker,* p. 16.

11. *Ibid.,* p. 144.

12. The prize was shared with Samuel Beckett.

13. "Books: The Author as Librarian," *New Yorker,* Oct. 30, 1968, p. 223.

14. *Ibid.*

15. *Ibid.,* p. 246.

16. *Time,* Vol. 89, No. 12 (March 24, 1967), 90.

17. See "Playboy Interview: Vladimir Nabokov," *Playboy,* XI, No. 1 (Jan. 1964), 45.

18. John Barth, "The Literature of Exhaustion," *Atlantic Monthly,* V. 220, No. 2 (Aug. 1967), 30.

19. *Ibid.*

20. *Ibid.*

21. *Ibid.,* p. 33.

22. *Ibid.,* p. 34.

23. Cited by James E. Irby, "Introduction" to *Labyrinths,* p. xxiii.

Selected Bibliography

PRIMARY SOURCES

The following chronological bibliography of Borges' writings consists primarily of book-length publications. Hence a number of short items—book reviews, notes, prefaces, newspaper articles, etc.—which have not been reprinted in his books are omitted. For a more complete view of his production, including original publication dates of individual items through 1956, see the bibliography in Ana María Barrenechea's *La expresión de la irrealidad en la obra de Jorge Luis Borges* (México: El Colegio de México, 1957), pp. 145–73.

The Emecé publishing house of Buenos Aires has, since 1953, been bringing out an *Obras completas de Jorge Luis Borges*. To date this firm has only reprinted part of his total production and indications are that their series will continue to be essentially a collection of selected works rather than a true *obras completas*. The nine individual volumes in this edition will be noted parenthetically after the regular title entry below.

1. Poetry

Fervor de Buenos Aires. Buenos Aires: Imprenta Serantes, 1923.
Luna de enfrente. Buenos Aires: Editorial Proa, 1925.
Cuaderno San Martín. Buenos Aires: Editorial Proa, 1929.
Poemas (1922–1943). Colección Poetas de España y América. Buenos Aires: Editorial Losada, 1943.
Poemas (1923–1953). Buenos Aires: Emecé Editores, 1954. (Vol. II of the *Obras completas*.)
Poemas (1923–1958). Buenos Aires: Emecé Editores, 1958. (2nd augmented printing of Vol. II of the *Obras completas*.)
Obra poética (1923–1964). Buenos Aires: Emecé Editores, 1964. (Augmented edition of Vol. II of the *Obras completas*.)

2. Essays

Inquisiciones. Buenos Aires: Editorial Proa, 1925.
El tamaño de mi esperanza. Buenos Aires: Editorial Proa, 1926.
El idioma de los argentinos. Buenos Aires: M. Gleizer, 1928.

Evaristo Carriego. Buenos Aires: M. Gleizer, 1930.
Evaristo Carriego. Buenos Aires: Emecé Editores, 1955. (Vol. IV of
the *Obras completas.* Slightly augmented edition of the 1930
original.)
Discusión. Buenos Aires: M. Gleizer, 1932.
Discusión. Buenos Aires: Emecé editores, 1957. (Vol. VI of the *Obras
completas.* Slightly modified and augmented version of 1932
original.)
Historia de la eternidad. Buenos Aires: Viau y Zona, 1936.
Historia de la eternidad. Buenos Aires: Emecé Editores, 1953. (Vol.
I of the *Obras completas.* Slightly augmented version of 1936
original.)
Nueva refutación del tiempo. Buenos Aires: Oportet y Haereses, 1947.
(A single essay.)
Otras inquisiciones (1937–1952). Buenos Aires: Ediciones Sur, 1952.
Otras inquisiciones (1937–1952). Buenos Aires: Emecé Editores, 1960.
(Vol. VIII of the *Obras completas.* Same as 1952 original.)

3. Prose Fiction

Historia universal de la infamia. Buenos Aires: Ed. Tor, 1935.
Historia universal de la infamia. Buenos Aires: Emecé Editores, 1954.
(Vol. III of the *Obras completas.* Slightly augmented version of
the 1935 original.)
El jardín de senderos que se bifurcan. Buenos Aires: Ediciones Sur,
1941.
Ficciones (1935–1944). Buenos Aires: Ediciones Sur, 1944. (Reprints
the stories of *El jardín de senderos que se bifurcan* with six new
stories.)
Ficciones. Buenos Aires: Emecé Editores, 1956. (Vol. V of the *Obras
completas.* Slightly augmented version of the 1944 original.)
El Aleph. Buenos Aires: Editorial Losada, 1949.
El Aleph. Buenos Aires: Losada, 1952. (Slightly augmented version
of 1949 original.)
El Aleph. Buenos Aires: Emecé Editores, 1957. (Vol. VII of the *Obras
completas.* Reproduces the 1952 Losada edition.)
La muerte y la brújula. Buenos Aires: Emecé Editores, 1951. (Reprints selected stories published in previous collections.)

4. Prose and Poetry

El hacedor. Buenos Aires: Emecé Editores, 1960. (Vol. IX of the
Obras completas.)
Antología personal. Buenos Aires: Ediciones Sur, 1961. (Author's
own selection of his favorite pieces, all in previously published
collections.)

5. Prose Fiction in Collaboration

Bustos Domecq, H. (joint *pseud.* of Jorge Luis Borges and Adolfo Bioy Casares). *Seis problemas para Isidro Parodi.* Buenos Aires: Ediciones Sur, 1942.

————. *Dos fantasías memorables.* Buenos Aires: Oportet & Haereses, 1946.

Suárez Lynch, B. (joint *pseud.* of Jorge Luis Borges and Adolfo Bioy Casares). *Un modelo para la muerte.* Buenos Aires: Oportet & Haereses, 1946.

Borges, Jorge Luis and Luisa Mercedes Levinson. *La hermana de Eloísa.* Buenos Aires: Ed. Ene, 1955. (Individual stories by each author; title story in collaboration.)

Borges, Jorge Luis, and Adolfo Bioy Casares. *El paraíso de los creyentes (Dos argumentos cinematográficos).* Buenos Aires: Editorial Losada, 1955.

————. *Crónicas de Bustos Domecq.* Buenos Aires: Editorial Losada, 1967.

6. Selected Miscellaneous Works: literary manuals, editions, anthologies, etc.

Las kenningar. Buenos Aires: Imp. Colombo, 1933. (A single short essay.)

Antología clásica de la literatura argentina. In collaboration with Pedro Henríquez Ureña. Buenos Aires: Ed. Kapelusz, 1937.

Antología de la literatura fantástica. In collaboration with Silvina Ocampo and Adolfo Bioy Casares. Buenos Aires: Ed. Sudamericana, 1940.

Antología poética argentina. In collaboration with Silvina Ocampo and Adolfo Bioy Casares. Buenos Aires: Ed. Sudamericana, 1941.

Los mejores cuentos policiales. Selection and translation in collaboration with Adolfo Bioy Casares. Buenos Aires: Emecé Editores, 1943. (Several additional volumes of stories have appeared periodically.)

Aspectos de la literatura gauchesca. Montevideo: Ed. Número, 1950. (A single essay.)

El "Martín Fierro." In collaboration with Margarita Guerrero. Buenos Aires: Ed. Columba, 1953.

Poesía gauchesca. Edit., prologue, notes, and glossary in collaboration with Adolfo Bioy Casares. Mexico: Fondo de Cultura Económica, 1955.

Leopoldo Lugones. In collaboration with Betina Edelberg. Buenos Aires: Ed. Troquel, 1955.

Manual de zoología fantástica. In collaboration with Margarita

Guerrero. Mexico-Buenos Aires: Fondo de Cultural Económica, 1957.

La poesía gauchesca. Buenos Aires: Centro de Estudios Brasileiros, 1960. (A single essay.)

Libro del cielo y del infierno. In collaboration with Adolfo Bioy Casares. Buenos Aires: Ediciones Sur, 1960.

Antiguas literaturas germánicas. In collaboration with Delia Ingenieros. Mexico-Buenos Aires: Fondo de Cultura Económica, 1961.

Macedonio Fernández. Buenos Aires: Ed. Culturales Argentinas, Ministerio de Educación y Justica, 1961.

Introducción a la literatura inglesa. In collaboration with María Esther Vázquez. Buenos Aires: Ed. Columba, 1965.

Para las seis cuerdas; milongas. Buenos Aires: Emecé Editores, 1965.

Literaturas germánicas medievales. In collaboration with María Esther Vázquez. Buenos Aires: Ed. Falbo, 1966.

Introducción a la literatura norteamericana. Buenos Aires: Ed. Columba, 1967.

7. Principal Translations in English

Labyrinths. Edit. by Donald A. Yates and James E. Irby. New York: New Directions, 1962. (An anthology drawn from several collections of Borges' stories and essays.)

Ficciones. Translation by Anthony Kerrigan and others. New York: Grove Press, 1962.

Dreamtigers. Translation by Mildred Boyer and Harold Moreland. Austin: University of Texas Press, 1964. (English version of *El hacedor.*)

Other Inquisitions 1937–52. Translation by Ruth L. C. Simms. Introduction by James E. Irby. Austin: University of Texas Press, 1964.

Fictions. Edited and with an introduction by Anthony Kerrigan. London: John Calder, 1965.

A Personal Anthology. Edited and with a foreword by Anthony Kerrigan. New York: Grove Press, 1967.

SECONDARY SOURCES

1. Books

ALAZRAKI, JAIME. *La prosa narrativa de Jorge Luis Borges.* Madrid: Ed. Gredos, 1968. Recent study in which both thematic and stylistic aspects of Borges' prose are considered.

BARRENECHEA, ANA MARÍA. *La expresión de la irrealidad en la obra de Jorge Luis Borges.* México: Colegio de México, 1957. A valuable survey of the main themes in his work, with emphasis on the prose. Excellent bibliography.

————. *Borges the Labyrinth Maker.* Edited and translated by Robert Lima. New York: New York University Press, 1965. English translation of item above with editor's notes appended. Bibliography of the original Spanish study greatly reduced.

BLANCO-GONZÁLEZ, MANUEL. *Jorge Luis Borges: Anotaciones sobre el tiempo en su obra.* México: Ediciones De Andrea, 1963. Rather critical and somewhat unsophisticated. Attacks Borges for his omission of human, social, and love themes.

CHRIST, RONALD J. *The Narrow Act: Borges' Art of Illusion.* New York: New York University Press, 1969. Highly acclaimed recent study of Borges' fiction and the first such work written originally in English.

FERNÁNDEZ MORENO, CÉSAR. *Esquema de Borges.* Buenos Aires: Ed. Perrot, 1957. Rather short schematic essay on Borges' total production. Neither highly critical nor highly laudatory.

GERTEL, ZUNILDA A. *Borges y su retorno a la poesía.* México: Ediciones De Andrea, 1968. A recent item just announced. Not examined.

GUTIÉRREZ GIRARDOT, RAFAEL. *Jorge Luis Borges, ensayo de interpretación.* Madrid: Ed. Insula, 1959. Interpretative rather than scholarly. Sympathetic presentation of Borges' sense of irony and caricature.

JURADO, ALICIA. *Genio y figura de Jorge Luis Borges.* Buenos Aires: Ed. Universitaria de Buenos Aires, 1964. Anecdotal and informal rather than scholarly, but has valuable insights into the man and his work by a close friend.

PRIETO, ADOLFO. *Borges y la nueva generación.* Buenos Aires: Letras Universitarias, 1954. The first book-length study on Borges and highly critical of him.

RAMOS, JORGE ABELARDO. *Crisis y resurrección de la literatura argentina.* 2ª edición. Buenos Aires: Ed. Coyoacán, 1961. Highly polemical anti-Borges views by a *peronista* critic. Also attacks Martínez Estrada, Sábato, and others. Original edition dates from 1954.

RÍOS PATRÓN, JOSÉ LUIS. *Jorge Luis Borges.* Buenos Aires: La Mandrágora, 1955. Rather partisan defense of Borges. Attempts to refute those who consider Borges aloof or "ahuman."

RODRÍGUEZ MONEGAL, EMIR. *El juicio de los parricidas—La nueva generación argentina y sus maestros.* Buenos Aires: Ed. Deucalión, 1956. On generational rift between young writers of the 1940's and 1950's and men of Borges' age. Also discusses Martínez Estrada and Eduardo Mallea.

SUCRE, GUILLERMO. *Borges el poeta*. México: Universidad Nacional Autónoma de México, 1968. A sympathetic study of Borges as a poet. Stresses relationship between his poetry and prose. Author emphasizes "intimate" quality of Borges' poetry.

TAMAYO, MARCIAL and ADOLFO RUIZ-DÍAZ. *Borges, enigma y clave*. Buenos Aires: Ed. Nuestro Tiempo, 1955. Emphasizes the prose fiction and Borges' technique of "dual characterization." In general, defends Borges against his critics.

2. Selected Articles

BARTH, JOHN. "The Literature of Exhaustion," *Atlantic Monthly*, V. 220, No. 2 (Aug. 1967), 29–34. Very provocative article on Borges and the state of literature in the mid-1960's.

BÉNICHOU, PAUL. "Le monde de José [sic] Luis Borges," *Critique*, No. 63–64 (Aug.–Sept. 1952), 675–87. Early introduction of Borges to French audience.

————. "Kublai Khan, Coleridge y Borges," *Sur*, No. 236 (Sept.–Oct. 1955), 57–61. A minor but interesting article on how a mistake in translation provided an erroneous basis for Borges' comments on Coleridge.

BORELLO, RODOLFO A. "Estructura de la prosa de Jorge Luis Borges," *Cuadernos Hispanoamericanos*, LV (1963), 485–94.

CAILLOIS, ROGER. "Avertissement du traducteur" in *Labyrinthes*. Paris: Gallimard, 1953.

CELA, CAMILO JOSÉ. "Buenos Aires o un mar sin orillas," *Indice*, No. 59 (Jan. 30, 1953), 2. Brief and general article by famous Spanish novelist. Some remarks highly critical of Borges. Part of a longer travel description, "Viaje al otro mundo."

DAUSTER, FRANK. "Notes on Borges' Labyrinths," *Hispanic Review*, XXX (April 1962), 142–48. A very sensible analysis of Borges' main theme of man's attempt to see order in an essentially chaotic universe.

DORESTA, VENTURA. "Análisis de Borges," *Revista de Occidente*, 2ª época, V, No. 46 (Jan. 1967), 50–62. A general survey. Considerable material on contrast between Borges and Kafka.

DURÁN, MANUEL. "Los dos Borges," *La Palabra y el Hombre* (Veracruz), II, No. 27 (July–Sept. 1963), 417–23. On Borges' "exorcism" of emotion and the duality thus created.

ENGUÍDANOS, MIGUEL. "Imagination and Escape in the Short Stories of Jorge Luis Borges," *Texas Quarterly*, IV (Winter 1961), 118–127. Suggests that even in his apparent escapism, Borges, may be writing about very real and very basic problems.

————. "Correspondencia: A propósito de Jorge Luis Borges," *Revista Universidad de Mexico*, XVI, No. 11 (July 1962), 31. Defends

Borges against the charge of "McCarthyism" raised by García Terres.

ETIEMBLE, RENÉ. "Un homme à tuer: Jorge Luis Borges, cosmopolite," *Les Temps Modernes,* No. 83 (Sept. 1952), 512–26.

FLORES, ANGEL. "Magical Realism in Spanish American Fiction," *Hispania* XXXVIII, No. 2 (May 1955), 187–92. Some discussion of Borges' relationship to this literary trend.

GARCÍA TERRES, JAIME. "La feria de los días," *Revista Universidad de México,* XVI, No. 10 (June 1962), 3. Criticizes Borges' political attitudes, but defends the journal's publication of an interview with him.

GHIANO, JUAN CARLOS. "Borges y la poesía," *Cuadernos Americanos,* XV, No. 1 (Jan.–Feb. 1956), 222–50. On the early poetry. Prefers this work to his more "presumptuous" metaphysical writings.

GÓMEZ DE LA SERNA, RAMÓN. "Sobre *Fervor de Buenos Aires,*" *Revista de Occidente,* IV (April–June 1924), 123–27). A very early review of Borges' first collection of poetry. Quite laudatory.

HART, THOMAS R. JR. "The Literary Criticism of Jorge Luis Borges," *Modern Language Notes,* V. 78, No. 5 (Dec. 1963), 489–503. Attempts to show evidence of a consistent literary theory in Borges. Points out relations with Croce and other literary theorists.

HERNÁNDEZ ARREGUI, JUAN JOSÉ. "Jorge Luis Borges y Eduardo Mallea," *Nuestro Tiempo* (Havana), V, No. 25 (Sept.–Oct. 1958), 9–12. On relations of the two authors. Also criticizes Borges' aloof political and social attitudes.

IBARRA, NESTOR. "Jorge Luis Borges, Poeta," *Síntesis,* No. 34 (March 1930), 11–32. Early example of critical view of Borges' poetry. Author states that poems written after *Fervor de Buenos Aires* failed to live up to promise of the first collection.

———. "Préface" to *Fictions.* Paris: Gallimard, 1951. Introduces Borges to French audience by stressing that he is essentially a "European" writer.

IRBY, JAMES E. "Introduction" to *Labyrinths.* Edited by Donald A. Yates and James E. Irby. New York: New Directions, 1962. Good introduction to Borges' fiction. Valuable comments on his biography and personality.

———. "Introduction" to *Other Inquisitions.* Translated by Ruth L. Simms. Austin: University of Texas Press, 1964. Excellent general comments on Borges, his themes, and the relationship between his essays and fiction.

KERRIGAN, ANTHONY. "Introduction" to *Ficciones.* Edited by A. Kerrigan. New York: Grove Press, 1962.

LEAL, LUIS. "Los cuentos de Borges," *La Palabra y el Hombre*

(Veracruz), II, No. 27 (July–Sept. 1963), 425–36. General survey of Borges as a writer of short stories.

LIDA, RAIMUNDO. "Notas a Borges," *Cuadernos Americanos*, X, No. 2 (Mar.–April 1951), 286–88. Praises Borges and notes element of humor in his work.

LIDA DE MALKIEL, MARÍA ROSA. "Contribución al estudio de las fuentes literarias de Jorge Luis Borges," *Sur*, No. 213–14 (July–Aug. 1952), 50–57. Rather erudite study of possible sources and parallels of Borges' themes in classical and medieval literature.

LUCIO, NODIER. "Contribución a la bibliografía de Jorge Luis Borges," *Bibliografía argentina de artes y letras*. Nos. 10–11 (April–Sept. 1961), 43–111. Complements the Barrenechea bibliography.

MALOFF, SAUL. "Eerie Emblems of a Bizarre, Terrifying World," *Saturday Review*, June 2, 1962, 34. Rather superficial review of English translations, *Labyrinths* and *Ficciones*.

MAUROIS, ANDRÉ. "Preface" to *Labyrinths*. Edited by Donald A. Yates and James E. Irby. New York: New Directions, 1962. Compares Borges to various major foreign authors, especially to Valery. Somewhat superficial.

MÉNDEZ, EVAR. "Doce poetas nuevos," *Síntesis*, I. No. 4 (Sept. 1927), 25–27. Borges lauded and included in group of rising young poets.

MORELLO-FROSCH, MARTA. "Elementos populares en la poesía de Jorge Luis Borges," *Asomante*, XVII, No. 3 (July–Sept. 1962), 26–35. Agrees with R. Lida that Borges' best work is his fiction, but gives sensitive analysis of the poetry. Stresses his fondness for late afternoon scenes and the note of "latent violence" in many pieces.

MURENA, H. A. "Condenación de una poesía," *Sur*, Nos. 164–65 (June–July 1948), 69–86. Penetrating remarks on general problem of literary nationalism. Critical of Borges and others for their lack of genuine national feeling.

MURILLO, L. A. "The Labyrinths of Jorge Luis Borges. An Introduction to the Stories of the *Aleph*," *Modern Language Quarterly*, XX (Sept. 1959), 259–66. Considers these stories an expression of the "spiritual crisis" of the century. Bears down heavily on this point.

PACHECO, JOSÉ EMILIO. "Simpatías y diferencias," *Revista Universidad de México*, XVI, No. 10 (June 1962), 32. Notes that there will be many "bad copies" of Borges' work, which he feels, should be a "terminal point" rather than a point of departure.

PEZZONI, ENRIQUE. "Aproximación al último libro de Borges," *Sur*, No. 217–18 (Nov.–Dec. 1952), 101–23. Ostensibly a review of *Otras Inquisiciones*, the author delves deeply and intelligently into the Argentine polemic surrounding Borges' value as a writer.

PHILLIPS, ALLEN. "Notas sobre Borges y la crítica reciente," *Revista Iberoamericana*, XXII, No. 43 (Jan.–June 1957), 41–59. Excellent review of the status of Borges criticism up to 1957.

———. " 'El Sur' de Borges," *Revista Hispánica Moderna*, XXIX (1963), 140–47. Close analysis of one of Borges' favorite stories.

REYES, ALFONSO. "Supuestos fantásticos" in his *El deslinde*. México: El Colegio de México, 1944, pp. 109–10. Section of Reyes' book in which the nature of fantastic literature is discussed with some reference to Borges.

RODRÍGUEZ MONEGAL, EMIR. "Crónicas: Macedonio Fernández, Borges y el ultraísmo," *Número*, No. 19 (April–June 1952), 171–83. Penetrating study of Macedonio Fernández' philosophic and literary concerns and their importance in Borges' work.

———. "Borges: Teoría y práctica," *Número*, No. 27 (Dec. 1955), 124–57. Excellent general discussion of Borges. Notes his strengths and limitations. Considerable material on his sources.

———. "Borges entre Escila y Caribdis" in *El juicio de los parricidas*. Buenos Aires: Ed. Deucalión, 1956. pp. 55–79. Discusses the attitudes toward Borges held by younger writers.

SÁBATO, ERNESTO. "Borges" in *Uno y el universo*. Buenos Aires: Ed. Sudamericana, 1945, pp. 21–27. Expresses an ambivalent view of Borges' work. His poetry more appreciated by Sábato than his prose.

———. "Los relatos de Jorge Luis Borges," *Sur*, No. 125 (March 1945), 69–75. A very critical review of *Ficciones*. Especially vehement in attacking Borges' "self-plagiarism."

———. "Una efusión de Jorge Luis Borges," *Ficción*, No. 4. (Nov.-Dec. 1956), 80–82. Critical of Borges' political views rather than of his literary work.

———. "Borges y Borges," *Revista Universidad de México*, XVIII, No. 5 (Jan. 1964), 22–26. On Borges the poet and Borges the writer of stories. Similar to item above.

———. "En torno a Borges," *Casa de las Américas* (Havana), III, Nos. 17–18 (March–June 1964), 7–12. Sharply critical of Borges' prose which is considered "tortuous and guilt-ridden." Continues to praise his poetry.

UPDIKE, JOHN. "Books: The Author as Librarian," *New Yorker*, Oct. 31, 1965, 223–46. As penetrating a survey of Borges' work as is available to English speaking audiences.

VIDELA, GLORIA. "Poemas y prosas olvidadas de Borges," *Revista de Literatura Argentina e Iberoamericana* (Mendoza), No. 3 (Dec. 1961), 101–5. Comments on lesser-known poems and prose selections of Borges.

———. "Jorge Luis Borges," in *El ultraísmo*. Madrid: Ed. Gredos,

1963, pp. 143–47. Valuable information on Borges' contacts with the Spanish *Ultraístas* before 1920. Reprints some of his poetry of this period.

VILLAURRUTIA, XAVIER. "Sobre *Ficciones*," *El Hijo Pródigo*, VIII, No. 26 (May 1945), 119. Shows early Mexican appreciation of Borges as a writer of fiction.

VITIER, CINTIO. "En torno a la poesía de Jorge Luis Borges," *Orígenes*, II, No. 6 (July 1945), 33–42. Reviews the 1943 edition of Borges' *Poemas*. General praise but points out the overly intellectual, prosaic character of certain pieces.

XIRAU, RAMÓN. "Borges o el elogio de la sensibilidad," *La Palabra y el Hombre*, No. 14 (April–June 1960), 81–90. Points out that Borges' stories are more important than his poetry, yet feels that his verse reveals much of the inner man.

—————. "Borges y las refutaciones del tiempo," *Revista Mexicana de Literatura*, Nos. 5–6 (May–June 1964), 5–11. Discusses the very basic theme of time in Borges' work.

3. Special Issues of Periodicals

"Discusión sobre Jorge Luis Borges," *Megáfono*, No. 11 (August 1933), 13–33. Many important writers give their opinions on Borges. Contributors include U. Petit de Murat, E. Mallea, A. Alonso, E. Anderson Imbert, and others.

"Desagravio a Borges," *Sur*, No. 94 (July 1942), 7–34. Statements in support of Borges following the announcement of his not being awarded the 1941 National Literary Prize. Contributors include E. Mallea, L. E. Soto, A. Alonso, P. Henríquez Ureña, E. Sábato, E. Anderson Imbert, and others.

"Los escritores argentinos: Jorge Luis Borges," *Ciudad*, Nos. 2–3 (1955), 11–62. A collection of articles and opinions on Borges by the younger generation of writers.

"Jorge Luis Borges," *L'Herne*, Cahiers paraissant deux foix l'an. 1964. Voluminous collection of articles, interviews, and varia by French, North American, and Hispanic writers. All translated into French.

4. Interviews (ordered by name of interviewer)

ALONSO PIÑEIRO, ARMANDO. "The Two Worlds of Jorge Luis Borges," *Américas*, XVII, No. 3 (March 1965), 11–15. A short interview contrasting Borges the man and Borges the writer.

BOTSFORD, KEITH. "About Borges and Not About Borges," *Kenyon Review*, No. 26 (Autumn 1964), 723–37. A "modified" interview: some very candid remarks by Borges along with Botsford's interpolations.

BURGIN, RICHARD. *Conversations with Jorge Luis Borges*. New York:

Holt, Rinehart and Winston, 1969. A series of revealing conversations between Borges and a former student of his at Harvard.

CHARBONNIER, GEORGES. *Entretiens avec Borges.* Paris: Gallimard, 1967. Series of radio interviews with Borges during his 1964 visit to France. In French.

CHRIST, RONALD. "The Art of Fiction: Jorge Luis Borges," *Paris Review,* No. 40 (Winter–Spring 1967), 116–64. Some very revealing remarks on how Borges began writing fiction.

IRBY, JAMES E. "Encuentro con Borges," *Revista Universidad de México,* XVI, No. 10 (June 1962), 4–10. Very informative: much material on Borges' personality, his literary gods, and the turning points in his life.

Index

Bustos, F., 90

Cabala. See Kabala
Caesar (Julius), 119
Cain, 99
"Calle con almacén rosado," 39
"Calles, Las," 31, 32
"Caminata," 33
Campo, Estanislao del, 62
Camus, Albert, 83
"Canción del barrio," 154n
Cansinos-Assens, Rafael, 15, 27, 60
Carlyle, Thomas, 68
Carriego, Evaristo, 14, 62, 70
"Carriego y el sentido de arrabal,"
  62
"Casas como ángeles," 40
Cela, Camilo José, 137, 158n
"Cercanías," 32
Cervantes, Miguel de, 81, 82, 85, 96,
  134
Characters (fictional):
  Albert, Stephen, 128, 129; Al-
  motásim, 76, 106–107; Ashe,
  Herbert, 101, 104; Buckley,
  Ezra, 104; Castro, Tom, 91–92;
  Cruz, Tadeo Isidoro, 133, 134–
  135; Dahlman, Juan, 118; Da-
  neri, Carlos Argentino, 108, 140;
  Eastman, Monk, 91; Finnegan,
  Black, 126; Funes, Ireneo, 94–
  95, 118; Ginsburg (alias "Gry-
  phius") 126; Harrigan, Bill, 91;
  Hladík, Jaromir, 100, 135–136,
  158n; Kilpatrick, Fergus, 119;
  Kotsuké No Suké, 91; Lönnrot,
  Erik, 118, 125–127; Lowenthal,
  Aaron, 133; Madden, Richard,
  128; Menard, Pierre, 91, 95–97,
  118; Mir Bahadur Ali, 106;
  Moon, John Vincent, 118, 120–
  122; Morrell, Lazarus, 91, 92;
  Quain, Herbert, 97–98; Rufus,
  Marcus Flaminus, 130, 132; Ru-
  neberg, Nils, 98–100, 101, 158n;
  Runeberg, Victor, 127; Ryan,
  119; Scharlach, Red, 125–127;
  Treviranus, 126; Widow Ching,
  91; Yarmolinsky, Marcel, 125,

127; Yu Tsum, 127–128; Zunz,
  Emma, 133;
Charles I, King of England, 42, 54
Chesterton, Gilbert Keith, 14, 75, 81,
  83, 84, 90
China, 128
Christ, Ronald, 151n, 155n
Christie, Agatha, 97
Chuang, Tzu, 80
Chumacero, Alí, 144
Cid, El, 14, 132
Coleridge, Samuel Taylor, 81, 84,
  134
Conrad, Joseph, 81
Coolidge, Calvin, 17
"Coplas acriolladas, Las," 62
"Creación de P.H. Gosse, La," 84
Criollismo, 55, 58, 59, 62, 63, 92,
  138, 141
*Crisis y resurrección de la literatura
  argentina,* 140
Croce, Benedetto, 66, 83
"Crystal Egg, The," 108
Cuaderno San Martín, 43–46
"Culteranismo, El," 67

Dada, 15
Darío, Rubén, 28, 29, 30, 57, 58
"De las alegorías a las novelas," 82
De Quincey, Thomas, 79, 86, 87
"Del infierno y del cielo," 46, 47, 49
Deslinde, El, 144
"Después de las imágenes," 58
Dickens, Charles, 68
Diego, Gerardo, 27
Dink, Miss, 14
Diocletian, 130, 132
Discusión, 55, 56, 70–76, 85
Don Quijote, 14, 66, 82, 85, 95–96
Donne, John, 87
Dostoevsky, Fyodor M., 83
"Dreamtigers," 88, 144
"Dualidá en una despedida," 39, 40,
  43
"Dulcia linquimus arva," 41
Dunne, John William, 84

"Ejecución de tres palabras," 58

DATE DUE

FEB 5 '80			
JAN 7 '82			
MAY 2 0 1983			
JUL 14 '86			
OCT 7 '88			
OCT 25 '88			
DEC 20 '88			
JAN 9 '89			
JAN 31 '89			
FEB 21 '89			
JAN 26 '90			
JAN 28 '92			
FEB 14 '92			
AP 28 '99			
GAYLORD			PRINTED IN U.S.A.